THE GUY
with *the* SIGN

Also by Terry Pluto

ON FAITH AND OTHER TOPICS:

Faith and You, Volume 2
Faith and You
Everyday Faith
Champions for Life: The Power of a Father's Blessing (with Bill Glass)
Crime: Our Second Vietnam (with Bill Glass)

ON SPORTS:

Vintage Browns
Vintage Cavs
The Browns Blues
The Comeback: LeBron, the Cavs and Cleveland
Glory Days in Tribe Town (with Tom Hamilton)
Joe Tait: It's Been a Real Ball (with Joe Tait)
Things I've Learned from Watching the Browns
LeBron James: The Making of an MVP (with Brian Windhorst)
The Franchise (with Brian Windhorst)
Dealing: The Cleveland Indians' New Ballgame
False Start: How the New Browns Were Set Up to Fail
The View from Pluto
Unguarded (with Lenny Wilkens)
Our Tribe
Browns Town 1964
Burying the Curse
The Curse of Rocky Colavito
Falling from Grace
Tall Tales
Loose Balls
Bull Session (with Johnny Kerr)
Tark (with Jerry Tarkanian)
Forty-Eight Minutes, a Night in the Life of the NBA (with Bob Ryan)
Sixty-One (with Tony Kubek)
You Could Argue But You'd Be Wrong (with Pete Franklin)
Weaver on Strategy (with Earl Weaver)
The Earl of Baltimore
Super Joe (with Joe Charboneau and Burt Graeff)
The Greatest Summer

THE GUY
with *the* # SIGN

And Other Thoughts on Faith in Everyday Life

From the Plain Dealer / Cleveland.com
FAITH AND YOU column

Terry Pluto

Gray & Company, Publishers
Cleveland

Gray & Company, Publishers
www.grayco.com

ISBN 978-1-59851-132-1
Printed in the United States of America
1

To Bishop Joey Johnson: So much more than
a pastor, he is a precious friend.

Contents

Introduction 1

THE RED BARN, THE SUPER BOWL AND MY CELLPHONE

A black-and-white lesson from the old Red Barn 7

Does God care who wins the Super Bowl? 10

Does gambling impact the joy of sports? 13

Screaming: 'Get off your phone!' But what about me and my
phone? 16

DEALING WITH THE TOUGH STUFF

Did a phone call change your life—and your calling? 23

Should you call a dying friend? Rocky Colavito
has some advice 26

It's easy to get stuck in the 'you owe me' rut 30

Is rejection a self-inflicted wound? 33

Do you try to impress the wrong people? 35

All those sports gambling advertisements . . .
How dangerous is it? 38

THE GUY WITH THE SIGN

Is the guy with the sign worthy of charity—or a con artist? . . . 45

That guy with the 'homeless' sign? Readers have ideas 49

Why are bad memories vivid, and wonderful ones elusive? . . . 53

Don't wait until tomorrow to start getting well 57

How can you show your faith at work? Do a good job 60

Things you probably won't hear in most graduation speeches . 62

PRAYER, HEAVEN, GOD AND YOU

Praying with a stranger on a plane 67

What are you afraid to pray for? 71

Will heaven open its gates for animals? 74

In need of a prayer? How about now? 77

A strange encounter on an early-morning flight 81

PARENTS AND US

My father did the best he could with what he had 87

The truth about our parents can be painful 91

Our mothers' dreams: Joy, pain and a thankful heart 94

My dad and the purple car 98

ENERGY VAMPIRES AND OTHER RELATIONSHIPS

Feeling tired? Energy Vampires are exhausting. 103

What does a woman want? Ask her. 107

How to 'make up' for lost time in a relationship 111

Haunted by the 'What Ifs?' 114

People Pleasers: Before you say 'Yes,' consider this 117

Tired of trying to fix someone else's life? Here's how to stop. . 121

Pets can help us cope 125

SO THIS IS CHRISTMAS

Christmas with my father at the Waffle House 129

Remember when there was no room at the inn in your life? . 132

Ghosts of Christmas past and hoping for a joyous present . . 136

CAN I FORGIVE MYSELF?

God may have forgiven her, but she still can't forgive herself 141

Regrets are powerful, but so is forgiveness 144

Should we 'cancel' someone when we disagree? 147

Can we really forgive and forget something so painful? 151

FAMILY MESS: WE ALL HAVE IT

Are you agonizing over your troubled child? 157
Instead of their last words, think of the life
    your loved one lived 160
Parents, read this regardless of your kids' ages 163
Are we playing the parent blame game? 167
When a crisis brings healing 170

THE CIVIL WAR AND US

In a roadside grave, a mystery about a Confederate soldier . . 177
Crossing Antietam Creek: Bridges to devastation as well as
    to recovery and forgiveness 180
The Fourth of July, a search for shoes and the Civil War 183

SPECIAL PLACES

Sunsets, God and Lake Erie 189
Finding answers in Michigan's Upper Peninsula 192
Far from home but closer to God 195
A scouting trip to the hills, a rushed wedding, a life lesson . . 197
A place that God created to remind us who's in control 200

SPECIAL PEOPLE

John Adams's funeral and looking for the 'Power of Today' . . 205
A teacher can change your life 208
Meet the Wayne Dawson you don't know 210
A voice from the grave: 'Be not afraid!' 217
The Arizona desert, Springsteen and experiencing God
    away from the concrete 221

Acknowledgments 225

Introduction

When the pandemic hit in the spring of 2020, my editor at the *Plain Dealer*, Tim Warsinskey asked me to start writing my Faith & You column more frequently—every week.

"People need something like this," he said.

I had been writing it about twice a month. It usually appeared in the Saturday paper. Sometimes, a bloodhound and a GPS was needed to find it in the paper. But all that changed with COVID. Warsinskey and cleveland.com editor Chris Quinn decided to move it to the Sunday paper, in a prime spot on the front of the Metro section.

Suddenly, the column found a new audience—people who only read the Sunday paper. It also received more prominent display on the Cleveland.com website. This was a bold move by the Plain Dealer and Cleveland.com in an era when many mainstream media outlets had moved away from matters of faith. It led to some criticism from those who "didn't want God in the paper." the *Plain Dealer* and Cleveland.com stuck with me and the column. I doubt most media outlets would have done that.

This is not a religion column. It's about Everyday Faith, which was the title of my first faith book in 2004. That was when I was still with the *Akron Beacon Journal*. When the *Plain Dealer* offered me a chance to come to my hometown paper in 2007, I would accept the position only if the faith column came with me. Editors Susan Goldberg and Debra Adams Simmons quickly agreed, giving the faith column a spot in a top 20 U.S. newspaper and website.

For several years, readers have been asking me to put out another faith book. The last one was Faith & You, Volume II. That was in 2012. David Gray is my publisher, and he thought the time was right for a collection of my faith columns, especially since it's now a weekly feature in the Sunday paper.

To introduce this book, let's start with what the faith column is not . . .

It's not about abortion, gay rights, denominational spats and other hot button issues. You can find zillions of stories and opinions about those topics. Often those are really about politics, and most people already have their opinions on them set in cement. Nothing I write will have an impact.

This book is called "The Guy With The Sign" because that particular faith column drew online readership numbers more like one of my Browns stories. It asked what we should do about those people we see standing on street corners, holding up signs asking for money. I still don't have a good answer, but readers had lots of opinions.

That's how this column tends to work. More questions than answers sometimes, and often the answers come from someone other than me.

I write a lot about people dealing with sufferings and "family mess." That term comes from my friend Bishop Joey Johnson of Akron's House of the Lord. Many parents are dealing with troubled adult children. Some of us have elderly people who are in our care, either living with us or in long-term facilities.

Coping with cancer. Coping with strokes. Coping with loneliness. Coping with the death of a loved one. Dealing with life in a nursing home. Wondering how to handle an addict in the family. These are my topics, events that impact a lot more people than many of the culture war issues that dominate the news.

At one point, Quinn mentioned to me that the faith columns were "comforting." I didn't set out for that to be the goal, but I'm glad it's the case. There is enough screaming, name-calling and shouting on the air and in print without me adding to it.

My columns come from a Judeo-Christian perspective. I taught the Bible and led services at Summit County jail for 20 years. That ended during the pandemic. Along with my wife, Roberta, and Gloria Williams and Luis McLat, I've been leading services as Akron's Haven of Rest since 1998. Am I formally trained? No. But I have a "battlefield commission," my early mentor in prison ministry Bill Glass once told me. Glass was a former defensive end for the Browns and a well-known prison minister for decades before his death in 2021.

Glass believed that people who write and talk about faith but who are "not on the payroll" of a place of worship are often more effective. They have to believe it—otherwise, why go into jails, city missions and nursing homes or become involved with kids through sports, music and other activities?

Faith writing is not a part of my job description. I do it because I believe God opened an amazing door in a major media outlet for stories such as the ones you'll read in this book.

THE RED BARN, THE SUPER BOWL AND MY CELLPHONE

A black-and-white lesson
from the old Red Barn

It has been years since I drove down Buckeye Road.

I was on Cleveland's East Side for another reason, but I began thinking about going to Benedictine High School.

And I thought of the Red Barn.

I thought of quarter hamburgers, 15-cent French fries. Add in a chocolate milkshake and it would cost a buck.

A buck for a burger, fries and shake on Buckeye Road in the early 1970s.

I wasn't even sure where to find the old Red Barn, which was a few blocks from what is now Martin Luther King Boulevard. Back then, it was East Boulevard.

I saw Orban's Flowers, still there. Some of my classmates had part-time jobs there.

I stopped at a spot. Looked vaguely familiar. The Red Barn is now a parking lot. I took a picture and sat there for a few moments.

I thought about our country now, and back then. Both eras have racial tensions in common. At times, the streets were angry and politicians on both sides often seemed clueless.

Then I thought of Wiley Pugh.

Suddenly, I had sense of peace.

Wiley Pugh was African American. I was a white kid who grew up with white kids in Parma and then Northfield. Wiley was from a middle-class family and lived near John F. Kennedy High School.

We got to know each other in home room, where we were sat in alphabetical order. . .Pluto then Pugh.

We also were in some honors classes together. It didn't take long for us to become friends.

I played (OK, mostly sat) baseball. He ran track. When our practices were over in the spring, we'd go to the Red Barn.

We talked about school and coaches and girls.

We both played for legends. Wiley's track coach was Gary Stevens, who later went on to be an offensive coordinator/ quarterback coach for the Miami Dolphins and the old Oakland Raiders.

My coach was Augie Bossu, who is in the Ohio High School Coaches Hall of Fame for football and baseball.

Coach Bossu rarely yelled. Coach Stevens was a walking megaphone.

"Don't you get sick of him screaming all the time?" I once asked Wiley.

"He's OK," said Wiley. "You get used to him. He's a good coach."

I later figured out Stevens coached Wiley (an average runner) as if he had the stuff to be a star. Stevens had time to coach everybody. . .hard.

Wiley liked that. He knew Stevens had a good heart.

That's something we need to do—look beyond the outside. Shut out some of the noise. Value what a person is down deep.

IT DOES GET OLD

I went over to Wiley's house several times over the years. We often played pick-up basketball in his neighborhood, where I was the only white kid in the game.

We sometimes talked about race, and on a few occasions Wiley told me, "That guy in the store looked at me like some (N-word) off the street, like I wanted to kill him."

He didn't use that language often. He shook his head as he told the story. I said something like, "That stuff gets old."

"No kidding," he said.

Because Wiley was a gifted musician and singer, he was a member of the Singing Angels. That was a way for both of us to get dates, very helpful because Benedictine was (and still is) an all-boys school.

No social media. No cellphones. It was an innocent age, at least compared with high school dating today.

WHAT DO WE HAVE IN COMMON?

The Red Barn food was awful, but we didn't care. It wasn't about the food. It was about who was in the booth with you, sharing the fries.

We could laugh at ourselves, and at the racial stereotypes.

We got along because we had far more in common once we got beyond the black/white, city/suburban lines that could have divided us. We talked about our plans. I was going to be a writer, a novelist. He was going into music.

Wiley graduated from John Carroll University. He joined the Air Force and became a radiation therapist, working at VA Medical Centers in Dayton and Cleveland. He died in 2014 at the age of 58 of a heart attack.

We lost track of each other as the years passed, but the lessons he taught me have lasted a lifetime.

There's a Kirk Franklin gospel song called "The Blood." My favorite part:

"Some say you're black, you're white. They question if you're real. . .Doesn't matter what color you are as long as your blood is red."

Two guys at the Red Barn about 50 years ago, talking about our dreams.

Two guys at the Red Barn who got to know each other because our blood was red and we never forgot that.

Does God care who wins the Super Bowl?

I have an opinion, but let's first go to the stats.

According to a survey by the Public Religion Research Institute, about 25 percent of Americans believe God does care about the Super Bowl.

And 49 percent believe God does reward players on the field.

I've seen other research that indicates a significant number of people think God has a stake on the outcome of games, etc.

That has led to this line: "God must really hate the Browns and their fans."

We can have a lot of fun with this topic, wondering why God seems to like some teams as opposed to those from Cleveland. At least, that was the case until 2016 when the Cavs and the Tribe both had monumental winning seasons.

But I actually thought about this for a while.

Most athletes at some point have probably prayed something like, "Oh God, please help me win this game . . . or get a hit . . . or make this free throw."

I'm guilty of that. But since I was a career .232 hitter at Benedictine (all singles), I'm not sure what that says about my relationship with God. I confess to having prayed for a little more than a .232 batting average for a few bloop base hits.

Does God care who wins games?

My answer is: Beats me.

My opinion is: I really doubt it.

In Matthew 20:16, Jesus said: "So the last shall be first, and the first will be last."

The NFL has tried to make that happen with its draft, salary cap and even scheduling. They are all designed to help losing teams. But with the Browns, it just seems they stay in last place— at least in the AFC North.

Jesus hung around with far more people considered losers by society than winners. He did have some friends with money, but most of his friends and followers came from the bottom rungs of the economic and social ladders.

When Jesus was talking about the last being first, he was referring to the Kingdom of Heaven. He was talking about those who sacrifice and suffer, not the traditional winners.

My opinion: God doesn't care about the Super Bowl.

Another opinion: You can pray for anything you want, including your favorite team to win a game. It's up to you.

So what does God care about?

I recently had this discussion with a friend. She is in the radio business and has a wonderful voice.

I would say the voice is "a gift from God." She didn't pick her voice, nor could she have done anything to make her voice sound as it does.

The same is true of Joe Tait, who was born with a great voice for radio.

Joe and my friend developed their radio skills. They worked hard for their success. But they started in a good place.

I really believe God expects us to make the best use of our talents.

In Matthew 25:14-30, Jesus tells a story called the Parable of the Talents.

A master has three servants. Before he leaves on a trip, he gives one servant five "talents," a form of money. The servant turns them into 10 talents.

The master gives another servant two talents. He turns them into four.

The master gives a third servant only one talent. He buries it in the ground, gives it back to the master and talks about how the master is a hard man.

The first servants are rewarded for making the most of their talents, the third is punished.

Athletes are talented. Some have more talent than others. Some waste their talents, others maximize them.

That's what matters to God. What do we do with what God has given us?

Does gambling impact the joy of sports?

When I wrote about the problems of Ohio legalizing sports gambling, I viewed it as a "one-and-done" project.

Sports gambling in Ohio is legal. That's not going to change.

I had my say about it, and the dangers of it. I doubt much will change, other than gambling will become even more mainstream. Cleveland.com is one of many media outlets running these advertisements to bet on sports, and that brings in money.

Pro sports once disdained gambling. It now embraces it. Point spreads and prop bets are mentioned along with batting averages and shooting percentages. You can bet on almost anything, anytime, anywhere—right on your cellphone—24 hours a day, 7 days a week.

This is not a story about the evils of gambling. Many of us know people who became addicted to and trapped in various forms of gambling. Nothing new there.

I received an email from my old friend and former *Plain Dealer* writer Burt Graeff. He mentioned a trip to Reno in the late 1980s with broadcaster Joe Tait. We were covering the Cavs. They had an off-day before a game in Sacramento. We rented a car and headed to Reno, "The Biggest Little City in the World." This was when Nevada had cornered the market on legalized gambling.

"We did some gambling," wrote Graeff. "You won something like 100 bucks, then treated us to dinner!"

Somewhere in the musty, spider-webbed corner of my memory, that sounds familiar. We played slots for an hour or so. We ate well. We walked around town. I recall buying some University of Nevada, Reno University Wolf Pack shirts to take home.

I also know some churches sponsor bingo games, and there probably are more than a few folks who gamble too much there. Gambling dollars seemed to have infinite destinations.

So this is not about how everyone who gambles is buying a ticket straight to hell or bankruptcy.

A DIFFERENT CONCERN

But my first column missed a main point, which several readers wisely mentioned.

As John Walsh wrote:

"I was watching ESPN's SportsCenter and they told me not only did Philadelphia lose to the Orlando Magic, but they added the statistical breakdown of how rare it is for a double-digit underdog who's losing by at least 20 points to win.

"So it's no longer just enjoying an underdog winning . . . it's about—you got it—GAMBLING! The focus on sports gambling is becoming what sports are all about . . . It's not 'Did you win?' It's 'Did you cover?' Or 'Did you beat the spread?' That's a numbers game—not a lot of sportsmanship in that."

Gary Sattler wrote:

"The overzealous advertising for sports betting and saturation is disturbing to me not only as a money grab, but how it distorts the enjoyment of watching pure competition and skill and leaving it as that."

My wife, Roberta, mentioned, "Your team can win and you can still be upset because you lost your bet."

That's true, something I didn't mention in my last column.

WHAT FOLLOWING SPORTS SHOULD BE ABOUT

I know, it's about the money.

Most pro players are multi-millionaires playing for owners whose franchises are worth billions. Money drives player moves from team to team, even teams moving from one city to another.

I'm not naive.

But the points raised by John, Gary and my wise wife Roberta are valid: Heavy sports betting can rob you of the joy of your team winning. It could be because your team didn't win by enough points—or perhaps you bet on a player to perform well and he failed to score enough points or grab enough rebounds.

Not only did you lose, it also cost you money . . . maybe very big money. That can have major negative ramifications in the lives of gamblers and their families.

WRITING FOR THE TOY DEPARTMENT

Once upon a time, I heard sportswriters "worked in the toy department" of the newspaper. Some of the grumbling came from news writers who knew we had more readers and avid fans.

The "Toy Department" comments were insulting. But there was a bit of truth to it.

I consider writing sports a diversion from real life, at least some of the time. You can mention a political issue and almost guess what someone will think about it based on party affiliation. We are a sharply and often predictably divided nation.

But ask, "Should Browns coach Kevin Stefanski keep calling plays?"

The answers will have nothing to do with politics. People with opposite views of the news of the day could end up on the same side of a sports question.

When the Guardians surprised baseball and won the Central Division . . . or when the Browns beat Pittsburgh . . . it can quickly bring people together people across racial, economic and political lines.

I love that part about my job.

Despite my high-stakes trip to Reno 30-some years ago, we don't gamble.

Roberta doesn't understand much about the different point spreads—and doesn't want to know about it. She wants her favorite teams to win and her favorite players to do well . . . period.

That sounds like true a sports fan, and you can bet on that.

Screaming: 'Get off your phone!' But what about me and my phone?

Walking through airports, people have bumped into me while staring at their phones.

Does this ever happen to you? In the middle of a sentence, people will stop, lift up their phone—and stare at the screen. Suddenly, you have disappeared as they furiously text. You stand there . . . forgotten.

Yes, cellphone obsession is more popular among the young. According to a 2023 story by Adiah Siler in Parents.com, the average teenager is using a phone for 7.2 hours day. Those ages 8 to 12, it's 4.5 hours per day.

Yep, they hook 'em early and hook 'em fast.

But my generation—those on Medicare—are also captivated by their cellphones.

At my health club, some people walk around the track, mesmerized by their phones. They wander from lane to lane, shocked when they nearly blunder into someone trying to pass them.

They sit on exercise machines, texting. Then they sit some more, scrolling. They can spend 15 minutes on a machine, not knowing where they are—lost in cyberspace.

I want to scream, "Just put away the phone and pump some iron!" Or, "Get off that bench, I want to work out."

But I know better. "Get off the phone" are fighting words!!!

For the record: I leave my cellphone in my car when working

out. I find enough reasons not to push myself physically at the health club without adding a cellphone to the list. I also know how the phone pleads for my attention, and I am weak!

WE LOOK HOW OFTEN?

According to research by something called App Annie, Americans spent 4.8 hours a day staring at their phone screens in 2021.

An article by Trevor Wheelwright in Reviews.org reports his organization surveyed 1,000 Americans 18 years or older. They came up with an average phone time of 2 hours, 54 minutes per day.

"The average American checks their phone 344 times per day (in 2022). That's up from 262 per day (in 2021)," wrote Wheelwright. "We used to check our phones every 5.5 minutes on average. Now, it's every four minutes."

A 2019 survey by an insurance company called Asurion reported it's 96 times a day.

Take your pick, it's a lot.

NO CELLPHONE? YOU FEEL A COLD SWEAT!

Here are some other results of the Reviews.org survey:

74 percent of Americans feel uneasy leaving their phone at home. (I plead guilty.)

71 percent say they check their cellphones within 10 minutes of getting up. (I plead guilty to this at least half the time.)

64 percent have used their phone on the toilet. (That's too personal to respond!)

61 percent say they have texted someone in the same room as them. (Not guilty, your honor!)

45 percent say their cellphone is their most valuable possession. (Not guilty, but I refuse to even think about losing my cellphone.)

36 percent say they'd give up their pets to keep their cellphones. (Wonder how many would give up their spouses/parents/best friends?)

Confession time: In the middle of writing this story, I heard a "ping" and stopped to check what basically was an unimportant text. I couldn't ignore it while working on this column. I did it twice!

LOOK IN THE MIRROR, CHECK YOUR EAR

Most of us who spend a lot of time on our phones know this can be a problem. We might dismiss the Bible when it talks about "worshiping idols" such as a huge golden calf (Exodus, chapter 32), but what about our cellphones?

"I'm deep in the house right now." That's what my friend Bishop Joey Johnson (pastor of Akron's House of the Lord) likes to say when delivering a sermon line he knows will make some people squirm.

As Jesus said in Matthew 7:3: "Why do you look at the speck of sawdust in your brother's eye and pay no attention to the plank in your own eye?"

Or in 2023, the Pluto translation: "How can you complain about the phone in your neighbor's ear when you have two buds stuck in both of your ears connected to a new Apple 14 iPhone?"

A REALISTIC APPROACH

Cellphones and texting are great for conveying basic information or sending someone a quick, positive message.

My wife and I went to a Cleveland State basketball game on a Sunday afternoon. We wanted to eat some Asian food and decided to do it in Cleveland's Chinatown. We checked our phones for reviews of a couple of restaurants, picked one and it turned out to be a great choice.

So this is not a column about breaking all the cellphones and everyone returning to communicating by smoke signals or letters via stagecoach and pony express.

But it can become an obsession. The phone pings, and we can't wait to find out who texted. When we text someone, and they don't text back right away—we wonder, "Why is that person ignoring me?"

Lots of research shows the negative side of extreme cellphone use. There is a theory now that some people can't talk to you in person or even on the phone. They want to text.

Texting can lead to misunderstandings. Sometimes, you type one word. The cellphone doesn't like it, and types a different word—wrong meaning.

You also can't hear tone of voice. A text can seem harsh when the spoken word might elicit a laugh.

Having the phone near the bed is a terrible idea. That's a consensus of most research. My phone is not in my bedroom at night.

A 2020 Psychology Today story by Anthony Silard reported, "More screen time causes increased loneliness, depression and anxiety and less emotional connection with others."

Most of us are familiar with texting and driving, cyber bullying and sexual material online.

The dangers are real.

But some of us have our own phone problems, even if they aren't as severe.

I set my cellphone early in the morning to check how much screen time I used. It's 8:40 p.m. right now. The answer is 1 hour, 14 minutes. I had no clue it was that much.

I thought I hardly looked at it. I challenge you to check yours, and you probably will be in for a not-so-pleasant surprise.

DEALING
WITH THE
TOUGH
STUFF

Did a phone call change your life—and your calling?

I was on vacation in the Black Hills of South Dakota when the call came from my aunt.

My father had suffered a stroke.

To my embarrassment, I didn't immediately come home. I was between shock and denial. I had seen my father the week before. We went to a Browns practice. Another day, we went bowling.

He was fine. A week later, he had returned to his home in Florida—and was in a Sarasota hospital.

Two days later, my wife and I were driving home. I talked to my brother Tom, who was with our father at the hospital. He then handed the phone to my father.

"Dad, how are you doing?" I asked.

"Man," he said. "Oh, man."

I was in a truck stop off Interstate 90 in Mitchell, South Dakota. This was 1993, before cellphones. I was on a pay phone, staring at belts and other truck accessories.

It was hot. I was sweating. My heart was pounding.

Over and over, my father just said one word . . . man.

That's when I really knew my life would never be the same.

TWO BIG DAYS?

"The two most important days of your life are the day you were born and the day you find out why."

Writer Mark Twain is believed to have said that, but scholars debate if he's really the source. I'll let them wrestle with that question.

The bigger point is this: Is the statement correct?

Are there only two days that stand out above all others? Hard to argue with the day of birth. That sets up all the rest of our days.

But the day you find out why? Only one day?

"I'd say it's the day you find your purpose," said Jeff Bogue, pastor of Grace Church in Fairlawn. "It's the day you realize God called you to know Him and make Him known to others."

Or as Rick Warren opened his book *The Purpose Driven Life*: "It's not about you."

Most of us know that, but it's not easy to embrace.

"The purpose of your life is far greater than your own personal fulfillment, your peace of mind, or even your happiness," wrote Warren. "It's far greater than your family, your career, or even your wildest dreams and ambitions."

Maybe the second-biggest day is when you discover it really isn't about you—even though down deep, you hate that idea. Or at least, that's how I felt back in 1993.

And I still feel that way when a phone call comes that seems to turn my life upside down.

THERE ARE SEVERAL BIG DAYS

I received this email from Nancy (her real name):

"Having just lost my wonderful and handsome husband of 49 years this past January, it put me in touch with the reality that I am not alone with the struggle of his immense loss—that individuals and families must go through this process when those near and dear to them leave us through death.

"It is devastating to go on without him and extremely sad. With the COVID still lurking, many churches and local centers are not open to grief counseling. The online sessions are just lacking the human interaction.

"The sharing of stories of the loss and pain of those we love and hold so dearly brings about a reality—we can appreciate that grief is just love with no place to go."

Just as getting married is a life-changing day, so is the day the spouse leaves or dies. Suddenly, you are alone.

"Your calling to serve God doesn't change," said Bogue. "But your circumstances will."

Bogue and I talked about grandparents who suddenly find themselves raising grandchildren because of a family situation.

"You wonder, 'I'm 60 years old, already raised my kids and now I have a 7-year-old in my house,'" said Bogue. "You never saw this calling on your life. But with God's help, you can get through it."

OUR LIFE, OUR CIRCUMSTANCES

My father's stroke led to the most challenging 4½ years of my life. Anyone who has had extended caretaker experience knows the feelings of fatigue, being overwhelmed and sadness.

But it also forced me to get over myself.

I know of people who have lost spouses through divorce or death. After a period of grieving, they have been able to help others in the same situations.

Following my father's death, I was part of a home healthcare team for my mother-in-law. There have been some other times when my wife and I worked with an elderly person.

Twain is right and wrong.

He was right about having a day when we see life and where we fit with God more clearly. But he's wrong because more demanding, frustrating, painful life-changing days are coming—until the last day of our lives.

"Our circumstances keep changing," said Bogue. "But our need for God and his power in those challenging times stays the same."

Should you call a dying friend?
Rocky Colavito has some advice

I received this email from Sean (not his real name):

"My cousin is my age.

"Although he has always lived in North Carolina, we spent a lot of time together while growing up. He even spent a summer with us in Cleveland when we were about 11 years old. We've stayed in contact.

"Recently I received a text from his wife, saying that he was diagnosed with a degenerative neurological disorder (very similar to ALS) and had at most only a couple of months to live.

"I called, and was able to talk to him. Even though his speech is a bit hesitant, the disease has not yet affected his mental clarity. But it was awkward.

"I did tell them both if they wanted to talk they could call me, any time, day or night. But I want to call them again. I thought perhaps you might have some suggestions, given your faith columns."

Of course, it's awkward. It will be that way, at least in the beginning. Sean's cousin is dying, and neurological diseases are awful.

Then I thought of Rocky Colavito, the former Cleveland Indians star.

I remembered what Nancy Score told me about Colavito.

He was one of the few friends who consistently called her husband (former Tribe pitcher and broadcaster) Herb Score in his final years.

Score had suffered a series of strokes and could only say a few words. But he loved hearing from Colavito, his closest friend for decades. They were teammates with the Indians in the 1950s.

DON'T WAIT TOO LONG

I called Colavito and read him Sean's email, asking for his advice.

"Tell him to call his cousin," said Colavito.

Colavito then mentioned a friend who had a series of heart problems.

"After a while, almost everyone stopped calling," said Colavito.

"He got some guys jobs, and they didn't even call. But after he died, they all showed up for his funeral and said nice things. What good is that?"

We both laughed, because it was painfully true. Why not tell someone what you'd say at their funeral while they are still alive?

WHAT TO TALK ABOUT

"After Herb had his stroke, what did you talk to him about?" I asked.

"Stories," said Colavito.

Colavito recalled when they were roommates in the minors. They had only one car. Colavito would drive Herb to where he'd meet a girl.

"I'd sit in a car and wait for them for two hours," said Colavito. "Then I'd take him home."

Colavito's point was to reach back into the past, find some shared experiences.

"Herb just wanted to hear my voice," said Colavito. "And I wanted hear his voice, even if he couldn't say much."

THERE IS A RISK

"Perhaps the hardest thing about any important conversation is opening yourself to disappointment," wrote Dr. David Feldman in Psychology Today. "If you tell someone how much you love them . . . you could always face the possibility that they might not return that love . . . so it's important to be prepared for a response other than what you want."

Colavito said he and Score were "like brothers, we never had a fight." Not every relationship was like that.

But in nearly every relationship, there are reasons to be thankful and upbeat memories to share. This is not the time to settle old disputes or demand forgiveness from the person. If there is something you want to apologize for, go ahead and do it.

But the real question is this: Why did you call in the first place? It goes back to what Sean wrote. He and his cousin have a long history, a good history. Focus on that.

Also, don't run from the illness situation being serious if the person wants to talk about it. Feldman suggests saying things such as: "This must be hard for you . . . Nobody can stay positive all the time. What's on your mind?"

Being honest is OK, as in this comment: "I'm not sure what to say, but I'm here for you."

Remember, the person is sick. There might be days when the person doesn't want to talk, or can't talk long. Don't take it personally. You can also send a text or a card.

PRAY FIRST, THEN CALL

My suggestion would be to close your eyes for a moment, silently tell God, "I'm nervous about making this call. I don't know what to say. I need Your wisdom."

Feldman also mentioned making a list of a few topics to talk about before the call.

The first few conversations might seem strained at different points. The illness hangs over the relationship. The next few calls will probably have both parties more at ease.

You also can pray for the person. You can pray for the health professionals taking care of them . . . for the person's family . . . for the person's strength. Ask first if it's OK to pray for them.

Score died in 2006 at age 75. Nancy Score passed away in January at age 85.

Colavito is now 88. In 2015, he had his right leg amputated below the knee due to diabetes. He appreciates calls from friends.

"Just make the call," said Colavito. "Don't worry about how you feel, or what could go wrong. That other person wants to hear from you—especially at a time like this. Just hearing your voice will mean a lot."

It's easy to get stuck in the 'you owe me' rut

"You owe me!"

Without saying a word, some people deliver that message.

You owe me because my father left our family. You owe me because that woman treated me wrong, or that man hit me.

You owe me because I was fired, or because I wasn't hired.

"When we are hurt, it's easy to blame others," said Dr. Diana Swoope, pastor of Akron's Arlington Church of God. "Some of the people being blamed had nothing to do with what happened to us."

We want someone to pay us back—even if they aren't the people who caused the problem in the first place.

"In our society, so much of it is all about me—my needs, my problems," said the Rev. John Lane, pastor of St. Paschal Baylon Catholic Church in Highland Heights.

The result is that we have a difficult time with relationships. Our conversations go negative, and we attract other unhappy people.

"This is not a popular statement, but no one really owes me anything," said Rabbi Stephen Grundfast of Beth-El Congregation in Akron. "When you are around a person who is so stuck in the past, you get tired of them. You can't change their past."

Most of us have "you owe me" periods in our lives, even if it's only for a few hours. I become very frustrated when there are problems with my computer or internet service, and my frustration then spills over into a discussion with my wife or someone who just happens to call on the phone.

I know, it's dumb.

But I do it. I write my long Sunday sports notes columns on Friday. A few friends call it "Grumpy Friday," and guess who is acting like the grump?

Is it the fault of those around me that I have a long workday? I sometimes act as if they're to blame.

We all unleash frustrations on those around us. But do we realize what happened and then apologize for these "You Owe Me" moments?

Obviously, some people have had traumatic childhoods, or they have been the victims of violent crimes, etc. Counseling is critical. It might take years to deal with all the layers of damage.

But some of us can help a bleak situation with a change of attitude.

"I have a family that is very close to me," said Lane. "Their father left his wife and kids years ago. They could have grown up bitter about that, but they supported their mother. They chose to be grateful for what they have, and they realize they have had a lot of blessings."

Lane talked about gratitude. He talked about service to others.

"One of the best things I did as a kid was work at a shelter and food kitchen," he said. "It really did make me thankful for what I have at home."

Swoope said healing starts with forgiveness.

"Suppose you are born African American," she said. "Slavery was real. Racism is not right. Things have been unfair. But are we going to blame everyone because I was born a certain color? Yes, there may be ground to be made up—but we can make up the ground when we forgive others and let go of all that anger."

Or as Pastor David Scavuzzo (Strongsville United Methodist Church) said: "God has forgiven me for so much. If I believe that, then I have the power of the Holy Spirit to forgive others."

Forgiving is not ignoring what happened. It's not restoring a relationship with a dangerous person. It is saying that I won't dwell on what happened to me.

"I think it helps if we admit not all of our motives and actions are exactly pure," said Scavuzzo. "And just maybe, we owe someone else something."

That could be an apology, or a thank you. Or how about being as patient with them as we'd like them to be with us? That's a good place to start.

Is rejection a self-inflicted wound?

You have rejection issues.

Very few things apply to almost everybody, but that does.

Think about it: Fired. Divorced. Betrayed. Not chosen.

And down deep, we hear a whisper, "Loser."

What causes deeper and longer-lasting pain: A broken arm or a broken heart?

Most emotional fractures come from the loss of a relationship.

You probably have heard the line: "Hurt people hurt people."

People who have suffered some rejection often reject others. It's an emotional preemptive strike.

"I know they'll eventually dump me, so I'll push them away first," we think.

People in the faith world would call this spiritual warfare.

"The thief comes only to steal and kill and destroy. I have come that they may have life, and have it to the full."

Those words are from Jesus, from John chapter 10:10.

That's why it's so easy to be sucked deep into the swamp of negativity.

Even great athletes have periods when they lose confidence. It's easy to see it in their performance.

Doubt leads to depression.

A priest named Henri J.M. Nouwen wrote: "I have come to realize that the greatest trap in our life is not success, popularity, or power, but self-rejection."

So often, we beat up ourselves before anyone else takes a shot at us.

In his book, *Life of the Beloved*, Nouwen wrote: "As soon as someone accuses me or criticizes me, as soon as I am rejected, left alone, or abandoned, I find myself thinking, 'Well, that proves once again that I am a nobody.'"

He calls it the self-rejection trap.

All of this is pretty grim.

Until we understand we have a spiritual enemy who comes to "kill, steal and destroy" our hearts, we can't begin to fight back.

Obviously, professional help is a good idea in some circumstances.

But this also must be fought on a spiritual level, through prayer and what I believe is the filling of the Holy Spirit.

I have periods where it seems a three-day old stinking dead fish has more life and meaning than anything I've written in a month.

I often receive dozens of wonderful emails. But a few come through calling me an "old hack" or a "journalistic fraud," and I find myself dwelling on them.

I have to hit the delete button. Then I need to stop and pray and be thankful for my job, my readers, my wife and my life.

Gratitude is a way to battle a bad attitude. Gratitude for those who love and accept us is how to pull ourselves out of the self-rejection trap.

Often, God has given us so many good things and people in our lives, but we need to look beyond ourselves to see it.

Do you try to impress the wrong people?

"I was just at the wrong place at the wrong time."

How many of us have ever said that?

Some may say the bombing victims at the Boston Marathon were at the wrong place at the wrong time.

Were they, really?

There's absolutely nothing wrong with running the Boston Marathon or watching it. The place. The motive for being there. None of it was wrong.

It was a random act of terror and evil that killed and maimed those people.

In my jail ministry, I often hear about "being in the wrong place at the wrong time."

Guys are arrested when a party is raided and drugs are found.

Or guys are shot when hanging out in the early morning hours on some mean city streets. Or they are in a strip joint when a fight breaks out, the police show up and customers end up in hand-cuffs, shoved into the back of a police car.

That's being in the wrong place at the wrong time—because there was no good reason to be there at all.

Too often, we go to the wrong place at the wrong time because we are trying to impress the wrong people.

My ministry partner Frank Williams sometimes tells the jail Bible class, "Some of us buy drugs from guys—and we take one look at them and wouldn't trust them to make us a ham sandwich!"

Teenagers and young adults often go to a party where they know there will be heavy drinking and probably some drugs. Many of them don't like the scene, but they go anyway—because others expect them to show up. And they drink more than they should.

Sometimes, the police are called by neighbors.

Wrong place. Wrong time.

Trying to impress the wrong people.

Suppose money is tight. Suppose some friends, with more money, want to go on a shopping trip. Suppose you know that fiscal self-discipline is not your strength.

Suppose you think, "I'll go, but I won't spend much. I just want the company."

What usually happens?

The mall can be as destructive to some of us as a trip to the bar for someone else.

In Galatians 1:10, Paul writes, "Am I now trying to win the approval of human beings, or of God? Or am I trying to please people?"

And I would add, "Especially people who don't really care about us."

A "friend" who invites a buddy with a drinking problem to a bar ("Hey, how can one or two hurt? You can handle it!") is not a friend.

A "friend" who asks someone on a tight budget to lunch at an expensive place and expects the person to pay is not a friend, either.

Why do we have an urge to please such people?

All of us know some very negative people, and we know where most of their conversations are headed. Too often, I fall into a trap, wanting to impress that person by topping his or her bitterness with my cynicism.

Or you might be drawn to a toxic, manipulative family member because you "want them to like me."

Isn't that another form of being in the wrong place at the wrong time trying to impress the wrong person?

Most of us battle insecurity. Most of us don't completely trust our own judgment. Most of us who say we have faith in God can find ourselves wanting the praise of the wrong people.

Proverbs 29:25 reads: "The fear of man lays a snare, but whoever trusts in the Lord is safe."

Why do I fear rejection by people who will never like me or care about me? It's a question all of us need to ask.

All those sports gambling advertisements . . . How dangerous is it?

I was listening to talk radio and the discussion quickly moved from the Cavaliers to betting on the Cavaliers.

It happened within 10 seconds.

The Cavs were playing in Memphis. Cavs star Donovan Mitchell was hurt. Would Cavs guard Darius Garland score more than 24 points? That was the "prop bet."

I thought, "No Mitchell. Sure, Garland will score 25 or more. More shots available for him."

Understand, I don't bet on sports. I don't bet anything. Period.

Confession time: Last spring, I got into a debate with a fellow writer about Steven Kwan. I had been a huge fan of Kwan since the 2022 spring training in Arizona. Keep in mind My wife, Roberta, saw Kwan in a 2021 Arizona spring game—a year before—and adopted him as one of her favorite players.

Anyway, my fellow writer said Kwan would end up back in the minors within a few months. A fair statement, since 85 percent of all MLB players go back to the minors at least once. I said Kwan would defy the odds. We bet a buck. I'd win if Kwan was still in the majors on my birthday in June. I won the bet, got my dollar.

That was my last bet. I can't recall anything before that.

Back to the point . . .

Listening to the discussion of Garland and scoring 25 points, I was thinking. "That sounds like a good bet." It easily could have sucked me into it.

What happened? Garland scored 24 points. The Cavs lost. I would have lost.

LEGAL BUT DANGEROUS

The point of the story is how the blending of sports coverage and sports gambling entices sports fans into the world of gambling.

While sports betting is legal, it's an awful idea for those of us in the media business who cover the teams closely.

Occasionally, I run into a fan who starts a casual conversation. Soon, it moves into specific questions about how long a certain player will be out due to injuries—or when he'll be back playing. Or when a team wants to rest some of its best players, as Golden State did against the Cavs last week. Didn't matter, the Warriors sat four starters and beat the Cavs anyway.

So much for inside information.

I know of two young sportswriters from a few decades ago who ruined their careers because they got deep into gambling on the sport they covered—and kept losing. They eventually lost their jobs and left the profession.

Now, sports gambling is legal. People no longer have to contact bookies and make bets in the shadows. It's all in the open, right on my cellphone. Ten seconds after I heard the discussion of Garland scoring 25 or more points, I could have pulled out my phone and made a bet.

Pure impulse, no thought.

All legal, but very addicting.

BIG MONEY BEING MADE—AND LOST

The onslaught of sports betting advertisements demonstrates how lucrative the endeavor is for those running the operations.

My wife and I were watching the Cavs game on TV. We couldn't keep track of how many different companies were pushing their sports betting operations—and offering "free bets." The other advertisements were for new cars/trucks and fast food.

Sports gambling is different and more intoxicating than many other forms of gambling. That's especially true for the audience watching the Cavs game and other sporting events.

We think we understand sports. We tend to remember when we were right about a certain player or trade—or when a certain team would win. And we forget when we were wrong.

We can be convinced to believe sports betting is more than "luck." We can figure this out—just like it made sense to me that Garland would score 25 or more points.

Yes, it was plausible, even logical.

But it didn't happen.

WHO IS THE TARGET AUDIENCE?

There is a lot of research now about how sports gambling is attracting young male gamblers, often younger than 40. They are not hardcore gamblers in other areas. But sports bring it on.

According to the National Council on Problem Gambling:

1. "Sports bettors exhibit far more 'problematic play'; indicators than non-sports bettors, including 'lied to hide gambling' and 'relied on others to pay debts or bills.' "

2. "Younger players (under age 35) appear to be at higher risk for gambling problems."

3. "Many people who gamble do not understand the way gambling works."

I'll add this: The onslaught of advertising makes it seem that "everyone is doing it," at least in the world of sports. Lots of former athletes are pitchmen for the companies. There are some betting parlors in arenas and stadiums.

IT'S ALWAYS THERE

I'm writing this as someone who learned how to read a harness racing form at the age of 10. My father liked to go to Northfield Park once a week, and he took me. He was disciplined. He set aside 40 bucks to bet, and that's all he bet.

He had to drive to the track. He had to study the form, walk up to the window. He had to pay cash. It took effort to bet. It wasn't done in seconds from home on a phone—and on a site that offered other options to place bets.

I've never been to the track since I last went with my dad about 50 years ago. But I do understand the appeal of a night out with some controlled gambling. Several decades ago, Cavs radio broadcaster Joe Tait and I would go to Reno on a off-day when the team was on the road. We'd eat at the buffet in a casino, gamble a little bit—and walk around town, people watching.

That's not what this story is about. Modern sports gambling is different—and far more dangerous. You can do it seven days a week, 24 hours a day on your phone. It's a constant temptation. One click and you can empty your checking account.

"Analysts and recovery advocates worry that efforts to research the long-term implications of legal sports betting and warn participants about the risks for addiction are falling short, particularly for people in their late teens and early 20s who are most vulnerable," wrote Marie Fazio in the New York Times.

I am begging parents, teachers, coaches and others to talk to their players about this—and I'm talking about young women and men in junior high and above. The goal of these companies is to bring in young people, hook 'em early. They already are living on their cellphones.

Please, take it seriously.

THE GUY
WITH THE
SIGN

Is the guy with the sign worthy of charity—or a con artist?

I received this email from Robin (not her real name):

"After church, a young man was standing right outside the door saying that he was homeless and hungry. I passed by him as I was speaking to another parishioner.

"I felt bad, walked to my car where I keep money in the glove compartment. There was only a $10 bill. I sat there deciding whether or not to give it to him, as he might be using it for drugs. I decided not to, and drove away the whole time feeling bad. Had there been a $5 bill or singles, I probably would have given it to him.

"I still feel bad and am reflecting on my decision. Why did I put a value on what he deserved? Why did I want to determine how he would use it? I give to organized charities monthly, why couldn't I give when it was up close and personal?

"I would never have missed that $10 and feeling foolish would be much better than the reproach I now feel toward myself."

Robin asked me for guidance.

I called the Rev. Jeff Kaiser, CEO of the Haven of Rest Rescue Mission in Akron, and read Robin's letter to him. He quickly said Robin was wise to donate monthly "to organized charities." He said a good way to help the homeless was to give to organizations that work in the field. I've also done a few fundraisers for the City Mission of Cleveland over the years. It also does great work.

There are lots of good organizations, including the Salvation Army, Catholic Charities and local places of worship that have outreaches to the homeless. I'm sure there are many others. A little research will lead you in the right direction.

"If you want to be sure your money is used well, charities are a good place to start," said Kaiser. "We can point people in need to different agencies and places that will help them if we can't do it."

THE GUY WITH THE SIGN

But what about the guy on the corner with a sign?

"A guy like that changed my life in some ways," said Father Bob Stec, pastor of St. Ambrose Catholic Parish in Brunswick.

Stec said a man approached him on a downtown street holding a sign and asking for money.

"Can you help?" asked the man. "I'm Jesus Christ."

Stec stared at him for a moment.

"How do you know I'm not Jesus?" asked the man.

It was an interesting question. The man could have been suffering from an emotional issue, really believing he was Jesus. Or he could have been saying that when you see the least among us, you see Jesus, as in Matthew 25.

Stec gave him $5.

"You really don't know the person with the sign or how they got there," said Stec, who carries extra $5 bills to give away.

NO STRINGS ATTACHED

If you give someone with a sign money, you have to understand it could be used for drugs or alcohol. Or maybe not. No way to know.

"We've had a 140% increase in overdoses in Akron since January (in 2020)," said Kaiser. "That really worries me. I know for a fact some of those are from people we see with signs, because of the work we do."

Kaiser understands, "If the Lord moves you to give to someone, go ahead and give."

But he also stressed the streets can be dangerous.

I've told My wife, Roberta, not to give money to people on the corner when she's stopped at a light. I'm not having her take any chances, especially after she had an occasion where she gave a man a dollar—and he began pounding on the roof of her car, demanding more money.

Others can make their own decisions.

IT'S TOUGH OUT THERE

I've seen some guys with signs scream at each other to secure prime spots to ask for money.

I've seen some men with their signs for years. Same men, same corners. Some of them probably can work, but don't want to deal with the restrictions of a job. Others are a different story due to physical and/or emotional limitations.

But I don't know their personal situations.

I once saw a few get together to figure out where they planned to set up. It was a meeting. They each had signs and cellphones.

Someone from our jail ministry told me how those guys coordinated with their cellphones. They pooled their money at the end of day. One guy had a car. It was like their business.

Sometimes, you'll be at a convenience store and someone will approach you with a gas can wanting money for fuel. "One of the oldest in the book," as one man from the Haven of Rest told me. If you want to help, tell them to go inside the store with you and you'll buy them something to eat.

WHO REALLY KNOWS?

I usually hand out dollar bills to some of the regulars. Some have emotional and physical problems and do need the help. Other times, I just give the money—and not worry about what happens next.

Not many women seem to be out with signs. I always give to them. I got to know one woman who was at a certain corner. She had a major back injury and other health problems. Not everyone is running a con game.

Sometimes, I will quickly pray for someone I encounter, and

remind them, "This is God's money." Most seem to appreciate that.

There is a man holding his sign, smoking a cigarette and sitting on a bucket turned upside down at the same intersection for more than a year. He also limps and looks as if his face has been used for a punching bag. I usually give him a dollar each time I see him.

Sometimes, I've given out extra pairs of socks. Most people love getting those. I know of someone who hands out McDonald's gift cards. It doesn't have to be cash.

"At St. Ambrose, people come in each week and make sandwiches," said Stec. "We have seven places where we deliver the sandwiches across the city. There are a lot of ways to help the homeless."

I don't have a good answer for Robin, other than working with charities is the safest and best option. To give or not give on the street, it's a personal decision.

ONE LAST STORY

I once was walking into a Circle K store. A young man came up to me. He was totally hammered, reeking of alcohol and marijuana. He wanted money. He recognized me from my speaking at the Haven of Rest.

"Let's go inside," I said. "Get some food, I'll pay."

We did that. Then I prayed for him.

About a year later, I ran into the man, who was in the drug rehabilitation program at the Haven of Rest. He reminded me of the Circle K store story, which I'd forgotten. He said that night was the start of his decision to try to get sober.

"You never do know how God will use you," said Stec. "That's something I've learned over the years."

That guy with the 'homeless' sign? Readers have ideas

I wrote a Faith & You column about the guys (they are mostly men) holding homeless signs and begging for money on corners.

That column broke the online readership record for my Faith & You stories. It was being read like one of my average Browns stories, putting up the same kind of numbers as my recent column on former Browns quarterback Brady Quinn.

I've learned people like to talk about this subject, even if they're not sure exactly what to say.

Many of the readers mentioned the safest and wisest responses were giving to charities such as Akron's Haven of Rest, Cleveland City Mission, Catholic Charities, etc. I'm leaving those comments out, because I stressed that point in my original story.

I'm turning this column over to comments from some readers:

OLD VS. YOUNG?

"I'm not here to judge, yet I seem to give freely to elderly people. Seeing the younger ones standing at my exit makes me think they can work."—Wallace

Terry's comment: I tend to think the same way.

"When I was in college, there was an elderly man sitting by the ramp near my school. At some point I decided to buy him a bottle of water, a sandwich, some chips and a candy bar. When I brought it to him, he cried and thanked me. He said he was diabetic and to give the candy bar to someone else. I still think of Mr. Henry 20 years later. I don't give money because I fear it could be used by on alcohol or drugs—the last hit to end their lives. But my children are used to me getting food and then going back and giving it to someone on the corner. They are always grateful and I've never been refused. Many times, I've driven away in tears."—Erica

SOME STORIES

"I was at work on Route 91 where a man in dirty overalls was asking for money. Went back a few hours later to Acme and used the bathroom. The guy was there changing out of his overalls. Followed him outside. He got into a brand new Cadillac with temporary plates. I just give to the Haven of Rest now."—Mike

Terry's comment: This story sounds made up, but I know Mike. It's what he saw.

"I once saw a woman outside a supermarket with her young son in the snow. I gave her $20. A few days later, I was in a restaurant nearby. I heard people talking about that same woman. Turns out, she wasn't homeless."—Jack

"I have a hard time with a guy standing outside a business where the sign says HIRING."—Joanne

"One day in downtown Cleveland there was a guy asking for money for food. I bought a breakfast bar for him. When I tried to give it to him, he said he was stuffed. So I usually don't give out money on the street."—Chris

"Y'all are terrible. We are humans, too. Not all junkies. Some like me just like to travel because it's a different walk of life. You should be ashamed."—Zac

"I was at Tower City with my Little Brother (from Big Brothers/ Big Sisters). A man asked for money to get something to eat. . .I reached into my pocket and pulled out a $10 bill. I thought it would be a single. . .I didn't want to give him $10. But I didn't want to put the bill back. . . . I gave it to him. . . . He thanked me and walked right over to Subway and bought a meal."—George

"This is not complicated. . .You are just not able to get over your judgment. Offer them food or bottles of water if you don't want your precious money used in a way that you deem unacceptable. Either you give wholeheartedly or you give conditionally—which is exactly what you are doing when you decide not to give because you think they might use it for drugs. You all are one major bankrupting, disabling medical disaster away from being on the streets yourself and you'll find it isn't that simple to get help or to get a job if you become unable to work again."—Erin

Terry's comment: I do think people have the right to decide they'd rather give water, food, gift cards, etc. Or to just donate to established charities . . . or volunteering in programs helping the homeless. But I also understand your point of view.

SOME INTERESTING SUGGESTIONS

"I don't feel comfortable just giving out money. I keep soft easy chew protein bars in car to be passed out. Bottled water is a good idea. A bus ticket is like gold."—Norm

"I keep small Bibles in my truck. I put a few bucks in each one. When they open the New Testament, they'll find the cash. Maybe it will plant a seed."—Scott

"I always give out McDonald's gift cards. Then I know it won't go for alcohol or drugs."—Mary

Terry's comment: These are all good ideas. Warm socks also are valued by most on the street.

GOING WITH YOUR GUT

"When someone approaches me for spare change, I always give them something and I always think, 'I'd rather give a scammer a buck than NOT give to someone who really needs a buck."— Donna

"I came across a homeless guy with a gas can. I gave him $20. My friends called him names. . . . About 15 minutes later, he found me. He tried to give me back $10, saying he didn't need that much. I told him to keep it and give it to someone else in need."—Bob

"You really don't know a person's situation even if you think you do. Drug problems are a sign of something a lot deeper.

Please be kind to the homeless. The last thing they need is extra judgment."—Ross

"No one demands an accounting of what I do with my money, so why impose a higher standard on someone asking for my aid?"—Tom

"I feel that when I help someone, I'm doing it because God put it on my heart. I'm doing what God wants me to do. If the person receiving it is a fraud, that's on them."—Terri

Why are bad memories vivid, and wonderful ones elusive?

The night I learned my mother died, I was working for the Savannah Morning News. I was on the phone, taking down information on a girls high school basketball game.

"This call is for you," a fellow writer told me. "Sounds important."

I quickly finished my basketball phone call, picked up the other line.

"Mom died," said my father, his voice cracking.

I was stunned.

I had been with my mother in Parma Hospital. She had suffered a heart attack, but was recovering well. I spent three days with her. She told me to go home, they planned to release her the next day. She never went home. About 24 hours later, another heart attack took her at age 58.

I left the newspaper office, made another 750-mile drive from Savannah to my father's home in Northfield. That was more than 40 years ago.

All of us have memories like that, heartsick ones that feel like they happened yesterday.

Bet you have some: The call into the office to hear about mass layoffs and you're on the list. The policeman at the front door with news no one wants to hear. The doctor with the grim face and the gloomy tests results.

THE FIGHT FOR GOOD MEMORIES

Why are most memories so painful?

Before trying to answer that question, a new memory came to mind. I recently was walking through the press room at the *Plain Dealer*. The machines were humming. Papers were still being printed, despite all the accent on the internet.

Then I remembered: My father delivered the *Plain Dealer* in the 1930s. First, he went door to door. Then he drove a truck, dumping off papers on different East Side street corners for kids to pick up and take to the homes of subscribers.

It was in 2007 that I came to the *Plain Dealer*/cleveland.com from the *Akron Beacon Journal*. I still thank Susan Goldberg, Debra Adams Simmons and Roy Hewitt for making that happen.

I now write for the paper my father delivered, the paper he loved—and I remain extremely grateful to the readers and still a bit surprised how my life turned out.

But as I write this, I had to work hard to assemble that good memory.

Meanwhile, the night of my mother's death . . .

The day I first spoke to my father after he had stroke and he could say only one word . . .

The times when I know I let someone down or embarrassed myself . . .

Those memories are vivid, like roaches awaiting the dark so they can crawl out from under the rug of our lives.

REHEARSING THE BAD MEMORIES

I was about 11 when we had a beagle puppy that ran into the street and was hit and killed a by truck. I clearly recall my mother going out into the road, tears in her eyes. She had a blanket and picked up what was left of the little dog. She didn't want me to see how "Flopsie" had been flattened. She and my father later buried the beagle in our back yard.

We later got another dog, a wonderful beagle named Pepper. I have to dig deep into the attic of my mind for some good memories of him. But when I do, it raises my spirits.

Often, bad events are branded in our brains, never to be forgotten. Good things? They are like brittle fall leaves whisked away in the wind.

Why is that?

A 2017 article in the National Library of Medicine by Deryn Strange and Melanie K.T. Takarangi opens this way: "Trauma memories—like all memories—are malleable and prone to distortion. Indeed, there is growing evidence—from both field and lab-based studies—to suggest that the memory distortion follows a particular pattern. People tend to remember more trauma than they experienced, and those who do tend to exhibit more of the 're-experiencing' symptoms associated with post-traumatic stress disorder."

The authors also said we tend to "rehearse" those negative memories in our minds. In other words, we dwell on them.

THE SPIRITUAL BATTLE

1 Peter 5:8: "Be alert and of sober mind. Your enemy the devil prowls around like a roaring lion looking for someone to devour."

There will be people willing to debate the existence of "the devil." But it's hard to deny the evil and negativity that tends to loom over us at times. How do some of our reprehensible thoughts or disturbing ones seemingly come out of nowhere?

I have written before about dreams that tend to repeat, most of them not pleasant. For me, it's being late for something . . . or losing something important. It's not a dream of a beautiful Lake Erie sunset.

There are times when I will myself to wake up and keep telling myself, "It's just a bad dream." I sometimes walk around the room, or sit up and read something uplifting, usually a faith-based book or the Bible.

In John 8:44, the Bible calls Satan "the father of lies." That explains some of the "battles that rage within us" (James 4:1).

In John 10:10, Jesus said, "The thief comes only to steal and kill and destroy. I came that they may have life and have it abundantly."

This is a war for our hearts, minds and memories. We need to fight it on a spiritual level, or we are destined to lose.

Don't wait until tomorrow to start getting well

Over the years, people have talked to me about their drinking and/or drug problems.

I begin telling them about Alcoholics Anonymous, Celebrate Recovery and some other programs that are available for free.

"I know that," they often say.

Then comes the discussion of how they "tried it. I was in the room with a bunch of drunks and drug addicts."

OK.

Or they didn't like the person running the session. Or the meetings were too far away . . .

Or too long . . .

Or too something . . .

THE BIG QUESTION

"Do you want to get well?" I sometimes ask them.

They stare at me as if I didn't hear a word they'd said.

But it's an important question. It's exactly what Jesus asked a man who couldn't walk and had been an invalid for 38 years. The story is in John, chapter 5.

It's something a friend asked me about 25 years ago.

It was when I weighed about 20 more pounds than I do now.

I was drinking gallons of regular Pepsi, eating lots of fried food . . .

And feeling like a slug.

"Do you want to feel better?" he asked me.

That led to a discussion of my diet, of cutting the Pepsi, most of the sugar and fried food.

Lean protein, fish and side dishes that weren't french fries was a good place to start.

THE EVIL INNER VOICE

I had to ask myself: "Do I want to get well?"

Immediately, a voice whispered, "That's too hard. Besides, you don't smoke or drink, you deserve your Pepsi and french fries."

That's how it works . . . we find lame justifications for not making the changes to get well.

Jesus asked the man that question . . . and the man had an excuse about people not helping him.

Then Jesus said: "Get up! Pick up your mat and walk!"

My version of getting up and walking was talking to My wife, Roberta, about a new diet. It was reading about what to eat . . . then actually eating it, at least most of the time.

And it was about changing workouts . . . and doing it the new (and a more painful) way. That was especially true after I had some back problems.

WHAT DO WE WANT?

In 20 years of weekly jail ministry, I've heard many addiction stories.

We have places for guys to go when they get out. Soon come the excuses why those suggestions won't work.

"If you looked as hard for a good meeting or church as you did for drugs and that woman, you'd get there," I often say. Most of the time, silence was the answer.

I read a blog from Dr. Michelle Bengston, who is a neuropsychologist treating anxiety, depression and many other mental health issues. She wrote how early in her career, she wondered why Jesus asked the man, "Do you want to get well?"

But over the years, "I realize . . . some people are more comfortable in their known discomfort than they are willing to risk the discomfort of the unknown."

ABOUT THE FROGS

When I have talked to people about attending meetings or even changing their diet, they tend to say something like "Maybe later."

Many years ago, I heard about a sermon called "Another night with the frogs." You can Google the phrase and find lots of material with that title.

It comes from Exodus chapter 8, the plagues of Egypt. It's where Moses confronts the Pharaoh about "letting my people go."

Lots of stuff happens, but Egypt is overrun by frogs. Pharaoh asks Moses to pray to get rid of the nasty critters.

"I leave to you the honor of setting the time for me to pray for you," Moses said.

"Tomorrow," said Pharaoh.

Think about it. Tomorrow? Why tomorrow?

Most of us would say, "Get rid of those bad boys RIGHT NOW!"

But it's so easy to say, "I'll start being more patient with people . . . tomorrow."

Or I'll call or text that person who needs to hear from me . . . tomorrow.

I'll go to the doctor . . . go to the gym . . . make that change. . . Tomorrow.

Pharaoh should have demanded Moses pray right now for the power to deal with the problem. It's the same thing we should do with our own frogs, assuming we really do want to get well.

How can you show your faith at work? Do a good job

Would I want to work with me?

There's a question that should be asked in every house of worship once in a while.

There are sermons about a lot things, including how to be successful on the job.

But would you want to work with you?

A few weeks ago, the answer was . . . no.

I had a meltdown with a friend at work. I started yelling at him on the phone about a problem—and it was not his fault.

I knew it wasn't his fault, but I was ranting anyway . . . and I threw in a few words that I hadn't used in 20 years.

After I hung up, I thought, "What a jerk!"

The jerk was the Man in the Mirror, to use a phrase from James 1:23-24:

"Anyone who listens to the word but does not do what it says is like someone who looks at his face in a mirror and, after looking at himself, goes away and immediately forgets what he looks like."

I did call back and apologize. My friend was far more gracious and understanding than I deserved.

DO IT WELL

How do we show faith at work?

I've talked about that with some people of faith over the years. They often move into the realm of helping fellow employees and customers when they are hurting.

But let's start with the basics.

"Do the little things well," said David Scavuzzo, pastor of Strongville's United Methodist Church.

I'll take it one more step: We should do our job well.

Bishop Joey Johnson (Akron's House of the Lord) sometimes tells his congregation: "If you are supposed to be back from lunch at 1 p.m., don't stroll in at 2 p.m. Show up for work on time . . . and be ready to work."

A person might want to talk to others about faith, but who wants to listen if the person has lazy work habits?

Someone once told me, "About 75 percent of good ministry is consistently showing up with a good attitude."

The same is true on the job.

HOW WE TREAT PEOPLE

"We need to work to see the best in people," said Father John Lane of St. Paschal Baylon Catholic Church in Highland Heights.

Gossip is everywhere. We can easily be attracted to negative conversations.

"It's best to keep those nasty comments to ourselves," said Lane. "They will come up. We will be frustrated. Taking a negative situation and adding to the complaining doesn't help."

Obviously, there are times when we have to face a problem. It's best to talk about the issue, not the person.

Name-calling can draw laughs, but it's damaging and should be avoided, period. Many of us can still recall names that stuck to us from childhood.

I was "Bucky" before I got braces. I had an excellent dad, but when he was frustrated with me, I was "Half-a-job Terry, that's what you are . . . Half-a-job."

I try to remember Philippians 4:8: "Whatever is true, whatever is noble, whatever is right, whatever is pure, whatever is lovely, whatever is admirable—if anything is excellent or praiseworthy— think about such things."

And when I fail, I just look in the mirror, then apologize.

A sincere apology is one of the greatest expressions of faith anywhere, on the job or at home.

Things you probably won't hear in most graduation speeches

Some graduation speakers are paid $100,000. Kent State paid that fee to actor Michael Keaton (2018) and actress Octavia Spencer (2017).

For the price of the newspaper (or free online), I can give some advice that at least won't cost much.

We'll start with some inspiration . . .

1. I have written more books than were in my house growing up.

2. I was rejected twice by the *Plain Dealer* for internships when I was going to Cleveland State.

3. It's big lie that we can do anything we want to. At one point in my young life, I wanted to be a pro baseball player. By the time I was batting .232 in high school (all singles), about all I knew about pitching was I couldn't hit it.

Now, I've been writing about big leaguers for more than 40 years, showing God's sense of humor.

But here are a few truths many of us at any age don't want to face:

Many dreams and careers have been wrecked by destructive relationships. That's probably one of those truths left out of most graduation speeches.

Just as important as picking the right job is picking the right relationships.

You want to go somewhere positive in life. You are dating someone who has a drug/alcohol addiction problem. Or they are angry and consistently negative. You think you'll change them because you love them.

You're wrong.

They are more likely to change you—for the worse. Most of us can easily see it when one of our friends is in a toxic relationship—but we don't listen when our friends warn us about an important person in our lives.

A huge reason I've lasted in journalism is I married on an incredible upgrade. Roberta is more than a wonderful woman, she is a Godly, praying woman. After 45 years of marriage, I still marvel at how God brought us together.

But we also dated for 3½ years before we were married. Our basic values matched. It was more than goo-goo-eyed love when we said "I do." I always believed there was a God, but didn't think God had much interest in my life.

About 30 years ago, I was struggling with how to care for my father, who'd had a major stroke. I was whining to a friend about that. He had been talking to me about prayer and developing a relationship with God.

Finally he said, "Terry, don't you get it? Life is hard. There is pain. You are going to go through it with God or without God. Take your pick."

I also had to face some sinful things in my life. No one likes the word "sin," but it's really selfish behavior. I needed God's forgiveness before I could forgive some others who had hurt me.

And all of us will be hurt. All of us will think at some point, "Life isn't fair."

And we know we have hurt others.

My main message goes back to relationships. Any graduate—any person—needs to work on their relationships with others.

And then realize at some point, most of us will be humbled and in enough pain that we have to look at where we stand with God.

My friend was right, life is hard. We are going through it with those around us, and then we need to decide if we want God to help guide us.

PRAYER, HEAVEN, GOD AND YOU

Praying with a stranger on a plane

I didn't want to talk.

That's what I kept thinking as I looked at the woman sitting next to me on my flight home from Houston.

My morning had started late in the evening—depending upon how you view getting up at 3 a.m. to head to the airport.

She was middle-aged, came on the flight with a slight limp. She had several carry-on bags that she stuffed under the seat in front of her.

She struggled to take off her jacket. I helped her with it. She thanked me about 47 times.

Then she pulled out a pillbox, grabbed a few pills and took them.

Next, she held up a plastic bag and asked the flight attendant, "Can you fill most of this up with ice."

She paused.

"I need it for my medication," she said.

The flight attendant complied.

We settled in for a long flight. I read for about an hour. She spent a lot of time looking at her phone.

I tried to sleep. So did she.

It didn't work for either of us, even though I sensed she was exhausted as I was.

Then she got up to go to the bathroom. She made it up the aisle and back, but she was unstable on her feet.

JUST DO IT

"Talk to her," I heard.

I'm not the kind of person who hears from God all the time. And when God does speak, it's a whisper . . .

A few words . . .

Usually telling me to do something I know I should be doing in the first place . . .

"How are you holding up?" I asked.

She smiled, nodded her head.

"OK," she said.

"Really?"

I asked that still not wanting to hear what probably was going to be a long story.

I was guessing she was a cancer patient flying home after being treated at a place such as Houston's MD Anderson Cancer Center.

And I really didn't want to hear her tale of pain and suffering.

"I've been better," she said.

She smiled. This obviously was a very kindhearted, quiet woman dealing with something very serious.

I heard the whisper again: "Just talk to her."

So we talked.

SOMETHING IS VERY WRONG

For years, she worked in a Houston hospital. She had risen up to be the head of her department.

About three years ago, she began having pain in various parts of her body. Then her speech began to slur.

"I used to be great doing math in my head," she said. "Then I couldn't add. I had a hard time talking. I couldn't think straight."

She went to various doctors.

"No one could figure it out," she said. "After a while, they were convinced I was crazy. It was all emotional problems. After they tell you that for a while, you begin to believe it."

She said all this in a soft voice, shaking her head . . . almost as if talking to someone else.

"Did they ever figure it out?" I asked.

"I was having problems with my feet," she said. "I was seeing my podiatrist. I told him what was going on. He said I should get tested for Lyme disease."

"You have Lyme disease?" I asked.

"Exactly," she said. "It just got worse and worse. I lost my job at the hospital because I had to go on disability. I couldn't do it. Some days, I couldn't get out of bed."

She said she was going to see a specialist in New York who had been treating her for the past year.

"They had to take me through the airport in a wheelchair," she said. "I'm only 41. I'm on disability. I had to quit my job."

THE SPIRITUAL BATTLE

"You've had a lot of losses in your life," I said.

Despite all that had happened, she had a sense of peace about her. She laughed about having to take all the different pills, trying to keep things straight.

She was divorced. She had a 14-year-old daughter. Her parents had moved into her home to help her.

"They are retired, and now they have to take care of me," she said. "I'm a single mom . . . "

Her voice trailed off.

"I'm used to being the one who takes care of people," she said.

She mentioned how it was "humbling." She felt like a child at times.

Then she began to talk about all the people who have helped her.

"There's a spiritual battle for all of us between being grateful for what we have and resentful for what we've lost," I said.

She talked about that in her own life, how it's so easy to dwell on the negative.

Will you pray?

A couple of times she mentioned how she was "embarrassed" by her speech and slurring words.

"But you're not doing that now," I said.

"That's because I'm going slower," she said. "I'm more careful."

"Not a bad idea," I said. "Proverbs 10:19 says, 'Where words are many, sin is not absent.' I'm a writer, and I keep telling myself that."

She thought that was very funny. She said the doctor in New York was helping her.

Soon we were going to land in Charlotte, both of us changing planes.

I kept hearing the voice saying, "Pray with her."

But I wondered if she was mad at God for what had happened to her. Or if she would be angry if I even brought up prayer.

"Do it," I heard.

So I softly said, "Do you want to pray?"

She nodded.

I put my hand on her shoulder and quietly began to pray for her trip. She took my hand and squeezed.

The prayer lasted only a few moments, praying for the people helping her, the people treating her.

"Thank you," she said. "I needed something like this."

"We all do," I said.

What are you afraid to pray for?

What are you afraid to pray for?

I heard that question asked once upon a time.

It made me think . . . just what am I afraid to pray about?

I know, you should feel free to pray about anything.

But . . .

"I know what you mean," said Jonathan Shaffer, the pastor of Grace Church in Middleburg Heights.

Shaffer said he has prayed for patience.

"And I usually ended up in situations where my patience was tested," said Shaffer.

Or praying to learn to love people who are difficult to love . . . and, wham, here comes a real grump into our lives.

Most of us really don't change unless there is pain involved.

"It seems like God uses suffering to get our attention," said Shaffer.

In my own life, I didn't get serious about my faith until I was dealing with my father's major stroke.

Father Walt Jenne laughed when I asked him the question.

Then, Jenne told the story of being in seminary and not bothering to study for a big test.

"I prayed like crazy for God to help me do well," he said.

And?

"I didn't do well," he said.

And?

"And that was God's way of telling me that I needed to study," he said.

Jenne talked to me not long after officiating at a funeral for "a perfectly formed baby that was born dead." He talked about the power of prayer in heartbreaking situations.

"I don't pray much for myself, other than I want to be a good priest," he said. "I pray a lot for others, especially for those who are suffering."

Romans 5:3-4 reads: "We are full of joy even when we suffer. We know that our suffering gives us the strength to go on. The strength to go on produces character. Character produces hope. . ."

When it comes to God and prayer, the more I think about it— the less I seem to know and understand.

Suffering often does produce strength and character—although most of us don't realize it until the ordeal is over.

"There are times when I've prayed for things and thought, 'That sounds really selfish,'" said Kevin James, pastor of New Community Church in Cleveland Heights.

Sometimes by hearing our own prayers and how petty or silly they sound, it's God speaking to us.

"I've prayed that God would make my children 'all that you want them to be,'" said James. "But then I add, 'Please have mercy in the process.'"

James laughed as he said it, but that made me think.

Pain and suffering often force us to look at our relationship with God.

"I've prayed for God to do whatever it takes to have this person get to know God," said Shaffer. "And I've been worried because their life is a mess when I prayed that—and it usually would get worse before it got better."

Don't ask me to explain all this. Prayer remains a huge mystery to me.

I have prayed for "God to use me."

Then I wondered what I'd do if I sensed God wanting me to quit working in the media and become a missionary in a place such as the Sudan.

Would I do it?

I'm thankful that I've never sensed that call . . . or maybe I just didn't want to hear it.

At one point, Jesus says to his Father, "Thy will be done," after asking if He could skip drinking "this cup" (the trip to the cross).

Sometimes, that's where my prayers end up: "OK, God, your will be done . . . because I have no clue what I should do. Just make it clear to me."

And God usually does, even if I don't like the answer.

Will heaven open its gates for animals?

Will there be animals in heaven?

My wife, Roberta, is counting on it.

Like some of us, she finds it much easier to relate to animals than to people. Her favorite job was working on horse farms, but she always battled allergies and eventually had to quit. Her allergies also forced her to give up cats as pets at home.

Animals in heaven?

"John Wesley, the founder of Methodism, believed that he would be reunited in heaven with the horse that had been his faithful traveling companion for more than two decades," the Rev. Scott Wilson, senior pastor of Mayfield United Methodist Church in Chesterland, said in an email.

"Having experienced the love of a number of pets in my life (even though the Bible gives no specific indication), I would not be surprised if they were near the front of the line to greet me when I get there."

Wilson and some other religious leaders I contacted mentioned Isaiah 65:25: 'The wolf and the lamb will feed together. The lion will eat straw like the ox, but dust will be the serpent's food. They will neither harm nor destroy on all my holy mountain,' says the Lord."

They say it hints of animals being in heaven.

"I am convinced there will be animals," said the Rev. Donna Barrett, pastor of Rockside Church in Independence. "Animals were an important part of God's Creation. He directed Noah to take them on the ark, two by two. God had a plan to save animals. Part of heaven is that we get the desires of our hearts, and for many of us, that includes animals."

Genesis 1:25 reads: "God made the wild animals according to their kinds, the livestock according to their kinds, and all the creatures that move along the ground according to their kinds. And God saw that it was good."

One theory is that there will be different forms of life in heaven, with angels being an example of something not fully like the human soul.

My friend Gloria Williams is convinced her 16-year-old dog, Spice, is part angel. I'm not about to debate the point, as it's easy to see something special in certain dogs, cats, horses and other animals.

But the presence of animals in eternity is open to debate.

Rabbi Stephen Grundfast of Akron's Beth El Congregation said: "Animals don't have souls, so it's hard to know if they will be in the afterlife. I'd tend to say not."

But he also said there is no way to know for certain.

"I don't know, either," said the Rev. Walt Jenne of Brecksville's St. Basil the Great Catholic Church. "Some theologians would say there are no souls in animals, so they won't be in heaven. But I also think there is a spirit about animals that is not the same as the human soul but could still mean they are in heaven."

Jenne said he recently blessed a friend's sick dog. He added that his associate pastor, Doug Brown, blessed animals on the feast of St. Francis.

"I was visiting someone at Fairview Hospital and ran into a man in a wheelchair," said Jenne. "He had a dog with him and said the dog was his best friend. I can understand that. I had dogs growing up, and I really grieved each time they died."

In his book *Heaven*, Christian author Randy Alcorn makes the case for animals in the afterlife. His point is that just because animals don't have human souls—and just because Jesus didn't die for the sins of animals—they still might have souls of another type. And if heaven in some way mirrors the Garden of Eden, there will indeed be animals.

It's easy for some religious leaders to dismiss this topic as trivial, but as Jenne said, "It's close to the heart of a lot of people. It does matter, and we should talk about it."

In need of a prayer?
How about now?

It was years ago when my wife, Roberta, and I sat down to pray at night. We remembered some people at church who were dealing with some significant problems.

"Was she the one whose mother has cancer or whose son is in jail?" I asked about one woman we knew.

That's when it hit me.

We talked to a couple of people after church about things they were dealing with . . . why didn't we just pray for them RIGHT THEN?

My goodness, it was after church but still in church. If you don't pray for someone there—then where?

Instead, I did the, "I'll pray for you later" line.

That said, I understand many people do remember to pray for someone later—and why they were praying.

I'm not one of those people. Many others would probably fall into the same category.

PARKING LOT PRAYERS

Obviously, there are times when it makes no sense to pray for someone. That's especially true if there are a lot of people around.

"If someone is talking about a struggle they're facing and I feel the urge to pray for them, I'll ask if we can step away from the group for a moment," said the Rev. Norm Douglas, pastor of St. Vincent de Paul Catholic Church in Akron.

Douglas calls them "parking lot prayers." You are walking out with someone, and before you leave each other, you quietly ask the person, "Do you mind if I pray for you?"

Douglas stressed the need to ask for permission so the person doesn't feel ambushed.

"I can't think of the last time someone refused," he said.

Douglas said he has prayed for a lot of people in parking lots. Or some he met on the street and they talked for a while.

"The prayers don't have to be long or eloquent," said Douglas. "And don't make them extremely loud. It's not about drawing attention to yourself when praying for someone."

And guess what? My wife and I could easily have done a "parking lot prayer" with that woman we talked to after church. That's where we all were going.

WHEN YOU HAVEN'T GOT A PRAYER . . .

One of my favorite songs is "Walking in Memphis" by Cleveland native Marc Cohn.

Why mention this in a column on prayer? How about these lyrics:

"They've got catfish on the table. They've got gospel in the air.

"The Reverend Green be glad to see you even when you haven't got a prayer.

"But, boy, you've got a prayer in Memphis. . ."

One of the messages is "even when you haven't got prayer . . . you got a prayer."

There are all kinds of prayers. Formal or spontaneous, prayer is talking to God.

"Just speaking from the heart," said Reverend Charlie Yoost, Director of Religious Life and Church Outreach at Lakeside Chautauqua near Marblehead. He also is pastor emeritus at Church of the Savior Methodist in Cleveland Heights.

Yoost said God has a way of sorting out what we're trying to say in prayer.

CLOSE TO THE BROKEN-HEARTED

Some of my favorite verses are found in Romans 8:26-27: "The Spirit also helps our weakness; for we do not know what to pray for as we should, but the Spirit Himself intercedes for us with groans too deep for words. He who searches the hearts knows what the mind of the Spirit is, because He intercedes for the saints according to the will of God."

I don't claim to understand everything in this passage. But it's the simplicity and honest emotion that God can relate to those "groaning" prayers. It's when we can't even put the meaning into words. Our soul is heavy, our minds are numb.

Psalm 34:18 reads: "The Lord is close to the broken-hearted and saves those who are crushed in spirit."

There have been times when I prayed like this for someone: "Lord, I don't know how to pray about this situation. But You know what is going on and what needs to be done. Help me to trust You and wait."

Or as Jesus once prayed, "Not my will, but Thy will be done."

TELEPHONE AND TEXT PRAYERS

"The pandemic changed some things about how I pray," said Yoost. "I have always preferred to pray for people in person. The pandemic forced me to do it on the phone."

Prayer on the phone can be powerful because it's so intimate—and also private.

"We simply have to do it," said Yoost. "You are talking to someone. You know they need prayer. Just go ahead and ask if you can pray with them."

Yoost is "semi-retired," but he has learned to set up Zoom meetings for talk and prayer. Text also is helpful.

"I know someone who lives out of state," said Douglas. "He is almost an introvert. But he's very comfortable texting. So we pray that way."

Douglas said there are times when he feels the Holy Spirit

leading him to text something encouraging to someone. So many people now prefer that form of communication.

Most people aren't judging how we pray for them. Many have been absolutely shocked when I offered to pray during a conversation. When I was done, they said, "No one ever did that for me before."

Prayer is a way to say we care, whatever the format.

"We should not limit the different ways we pray," said Douglas. "And when the opportunity is there to pray—don't worry, just go ahead and do it."

A strange encounter on an early-morning flight

It was an early-morning flight to Charlotte.

I was settled into an aisle seat and a woman in her 20s said she was sitting in the window seat next to me.

She was wearing very short shorts and a halter top and she looked exhausted. She had lots of tattoos.

"Did you spend the night in the airport, too?" she asked.

I didn't.

As the morning sun was rising outside the jet window, she then told me a long story. It was about bad weather, canceled flights, drinking a few Long Island Iced Teas and sleeping near the gate where we boarded the plane.

I listened sympathetically. I've been there—other than the Long Island Iced Tea part.

Her only luggage was a small backpack. We talked for a while about where we were going. I was headed to Atlanta to cover the Cavaliers. She was going to Charlotte "for a few meetings."

I nodded.

She told me that she was helping to support her mother. She was estranged from her father. "He's real religious and he doesn't like my tattoos."

I nodded again.

She talked about her best friend, "my brother." She said he was doing more than 20 years at a prison in southern Ohio.

I told her about being in weekly jail ministry. I told her to encourage her brother to connect at that prison for Bible studies and weekly services.

She said she prayed for her brother and missed him so much.

"My best friend," she said again.

"I was going to take my friend with me today," she said. "But I walked in on her doing heroin—with a needle. Ever see anyone shoot up like that before? I never did. IT FREAKED ME RIGHT OUT."

"Sounds bad," I said.

"I couldn't take her," she said.

We both agreed her friend needed help. I mentioned the Harvest Home for women at the Haven of Rest in Akron. A lot of people have been helped by that city mission.

"Guess I should just tell you," she said. "I'm in the escort business."

That explained her "meetings" in Charlotte. She was going to two different cut-rate hotels near the Charlotte airport.

At that point, I silently prayed, "All right, Lord, what am I supposed to say now?"

I thought of Jesus and how he dealt with women who found themselves in the same position as the young lady next to me. I told myself to keep looking at her eyes, not her halter top. I prayed for something to say.

She told me how the money "was good," and that she had no intention of leaving the escort business. I saw no reason to debate that point with her.

Finally, I told her that God loved her and didn't want her being abused or pushed around.

She nodded, but was digging through her backpack. Suddenly, she was almost manic.

"I wanted to give you my business card," she said.

"That's OK," I said. "I've been married 37 years and Roberta is my best friend. I wouldn't take it."

"Most of the guys I know say marriage doesn't work," she said.

"I bet," I said. "It could be that you're meeting the wrong kind of guys."

"You got that right," she said, laughing.

She grabbed her backpack again, digging through it. She was beginning to panic.

"I lost my wallet," she said. "What am I going to do?"

At first, I thought this was the "I lost my wallet, give me some money hustle."

But she was starting to cry. She said, "I know it's back at the airport. Probably fell out when I was sleeping. Maybe someone took it."

I told her that when we landed in Charlotte, I'd help her talk to a gate agent. That person could call back to the Akron airport.

We did that after our flight landed. She was a mess, and together we talked to the gate agent, who promised to make some calls for her.

She sat down, waiting, tears dripping down her face.

"I have about 30 minutes to get to my flight," I said. "Let me pray with you."

I put my hand on her shoulder, prayed for her lost wallet, for her brother and for her.

"I do pray sometimes," she said.

"That's good," I said. "Keep it up. It doesn't always feel like it, but God does love you."

She still hadn't asked for money. I gave her some. She started to cry again.

"God has more for you than this," I said.

"I hope so," she said.

"He does," I said.

PARENTS
AND US

My father did the best he could with what he had

What do you think when you look at your father's tombstone?

It's a dangerous and painful question for many of us whose fathers had problems. Some of us might not even know what happened to our biological fathers.

Those of us who are fathers can become frightened when we turn that question around: What will our children think when they look at our tombstone?

It's a scary question on Father's Day, but one worth asking. That's especially true for those of us who still have time to nurture relationships with our children, regardless of their age.

I'd settle for this answer: My father did the best he could with what he had.

That's what I thought when I visited my parents' grave last weekend at All Saints Cemetery in Northfield.

HUSBAND

TOM C. JR.

FEB 11, 1920

FEB 11, 1998.

My mother died in 1984. My father picked out the grave site and tombstone. He kept it small and brief. He was like that. Why waste the money? He wasn't going to be around to see his own tombstone, right?

As I stared at my father's tombstone, I said a prayer of thanks for having a father who remained in my life.

He could be moody and sarcastic, or fall into long periods of silence. But he always was there . . . a man of his word. My father wasn't always on time, he was perpetually 10 minutes early. I always knew I could count on him, perhaps the best blessing he gave me.

He hated credit cards.

He poisoned me against drinking: "I work at the warehouse with all these jakes. They get paid Friday, stop at the bar and leave half their paychecks there before they get home."

Every Sunday he took me to church. My mother seldom went. They were from two different religious backgrounds.

As we headed to church, he wore a fedora hat, a dress shirt and tie.

"You put money in the (collection) basket, you be thankful," he'd say.

It was just like he went to work every day and was grateful for it, even though he sometimes hated his job.

BORN 100 YEARS AGO

In 2020, I looked at my father's grave. I didn't dwell on the fact he died exactly on his 78th birthday after a nearly five-year battle that began after a major stroke. Instead, I thought about him being born a century ago: February 11, 1920.

He was born during spring training in a year the Indians went on to win the World Series. He wasn't old enough to go to his beloved League Park.

He became a Tribe fan in the 1930s, when the Depression not only flattened the economy but also his favorite baseball team. He took a street car to see the Indians. He was a member of the "Knot Hole Gang" of kids who watched the games through holes in the fence.

My mother and father argued a lot about money. She liked to spend. He didn't.

"You are going to drive us into the poorhouse," he yelled at her when I was a kid in the 1960s.

At the time, I didn't realize he had lived through 25 percent unemployment and "long soup lines" as he called them.

He was in the Army during World War II. He never went overseas, but traveled to bases from Maryland to Washington state to California. He worked in what he called "reconditioning" with soldiers who came home and were recovering from their wounds.

He loved Santa Barbara and wanted to stay in California after the war. But his family was in Cleveland. He knew he could get a job in Cleveland. He was shaped by the Depression, World War II and growing up in a Slovak home where English was a second language. He didn't want to take any chances in California.

MY FATHER'S DREAM

Several years ago, I received an email from a friend who saw a 1940 Benedictine High School yearbook.

It read: "Tom's pass-snaring in the Parma game climaxed his football career. By the way, Tom, don't forget to give the Bengals a blow when you become sports editor of the Press. What a slick blue buggy you've got, Tom."

My father loved sports and played a summer of Class D independent minor-league baseball in West Virginia before enlisting in the Army. He also played on some teams with major leaguers when in the Army. He always told me, "You have no idea how good those guys are."

He was so proud of my older brother, Tom, who was a terrific baseball player at Benedictine and later a coach at Cleveland Central Catholic.

My father worked at the old Fisher-Fazio grocery company warehouse. I also had summer jobs there for a few years. He wanted me to learn the world of hard work at an early age.

He took me to Indians games. We'd listen to Pete Franklin doing his pregame "clubhouse confidential" show on the radio. Then we'd listen to Franklin's postgame show on the way home. He loved Franklin.

We'd play catch in the backyard. He'd fall asleep on the couch watching baseball on TV. His snoring made the walls of our small Parma home shake.

HE WAS THE FOUNDATION

He told me about getting up early in the morning to deliver the *Plain Dealer* in the 1930s. But he never said a word about wanting to write or work for the Cleveland Press.

I came along in 1955, so perhaps by then his life was set. A steady job was about all he could expect.

My father watched me become a sportswriter in Cleveland. He wasn't one to say, "I'm proud of you," but I knew it was true.

As I stood over my father's grave, I remembered when I was small and going to Tribe games. We'd walk down the West 3rd Street Bridge to the old Cleveland Stadium. He'd put me up on his shoulders so I could see the ballpark and Lake Erie in the distance.

Even 22 years after his death, I still feel like I'm on his shoulders. He gave me the life he never could have had—and I'm grateful for it.

The truth about our parents can be painful

"I now realize my father is a fraud."

That letter came from a man in his 30s. He has been dealing with some personal problems, and also looking at his life.

His father had some iffy business dealings. He had several broken relationships. He "lived on credit cards for years."

What the son is trying to do is to have a realistic view of his father—but not be bitter.

When we have our own struggles, the temptation is to stare into the rear-view mirror of life and look for a reason.

Often, the figures looming large are our parents.

When we're teenagers, some of us go through a period where we're embarrassed to be in the same room as our parents—at least when our friends are around.

But this is different.

It's realizing we are now adults. It's knowing our parents did have an impact on us.

It's a tendency to compare our parental situation with that of our friends. Often, they seemed to get a better deal almost from the moment of birth.

Of course, we might have a different opinion if we had grown up with their parents.

Then it's facing this question: Will I grow up to be like the parent who so disappointed me?

That's a critical question.

Are we doomed to repeat their failures?

Or are we destined to not live up to their standards?

The letter writer never became the athlete that his father hoped.

Hey, that was also true in my family. My father played a year of Class D minor league baseball before World War II.

My father was a very good athlete at Benedictine. So was my brother.

I was on teams in high school and even one year in college. I spent most of the time sitting on various benches and watching games. Now I see that as great training for my long career as a sportswriter.

Back then, it was painful to see my father come to games and I didn't play.

Now, I'm grateful he came and he cared.

I'm also thankful I was not an exceptional athlete because those careers are so short. High-level athletes often have trouble coping with the real world, especially when the games end.

Big Truth: In some way, all of us will let down our parents.

Another Truth: Even the best parents will disappoint us at some point.

I had written the younger man about how our heavenly father is not like our earthly fathers. We often confuse them, especially if we had a very hard, judgmental father.

Or an untrustworthy father. Or a father who abandoned us.

It's tempting to view God the same way.

He wrote by reading and studying some of the Psalms in the Bible, "I realize my heavenly father is not a fraud."

The older I get, the more I appreciate both of my parents. My mother was loving and encouraging. My father was steady and disciplined.

They had flaws and a sometimes volatile marriage, but many of my friends would have loved to have had parents like them.

For others, we just have to realize we might have been wounded by our parents . . . and it's painful . . . but not fatal.

I suggested the man study Psalm 103, especially verses 8-10.

It starts, "The Lord is compassionate and gracious, slow to anger and abounding in love. He will not always accuse, nor will he harbor his anger forever."

Like many children, he also felt he let his dad down in some ways.

"Now, I realize my life is my own," the man wrote me. "With God at my side, I can deal with the struggles. I can work things through. I can lean on him for guidance."

Our mothers' dreams: Joy, pain and a thankful heart

As I write this, I'm staring at an old black and white photo of my mother playing a piano.

Or at least, I always thought it was a piano until I looked closely just now.

It's an organ.

My mother appears to be in her early 20s. Maybe younger. Her smile is radiant. She is happy and at peace at the keyboard.

I never knew my mother played an organ. Once in a while, she talked about playing the piano—but I never saw or heard her do it. We never had a piano in our house.

She grew up on the East Side of Cleveland, near Benedictine High. Both of her parents were from Slovakia. Her father (my grandfather) often told me of "graduating from third grade in the old country."

He was proud of it. They celebrated by eating "big hot dogs." I doubt my grandmother went to school at all. My mother went to John Adams High School, where she apparently learned the piano.

I do know she played the piano. I've received a few emails from people who knew her. Some mentioned it at her funeral in 1984.

She once said something about going to Oberlin to study music, but that memory is foggy.

I do know my mother had dreams. Every mom does. Some talk about them. Others don't.

And I wish I had taken the time to talk to her about those dreams once I started to have dreams of my own.

But I never did.

So why bring this up on Mother's Day weekend?

My mother died in 1984 of a heart attack at age 58. I was 29, meaning I have lived longer without her (38 years) than with her (29).

From that immigrant family, how did she learn the piano? What did her old-world parents think? It's probably a good story that I missed.

A PAINFUL BIRTH

This is the day to thank God and your "mom" for what meant the most to you.

My mother often told me, "You were a surprise."

She said that with a smile. She said that because I was born 10 years after my brother. She said that because she thought there would be no more children. She wanted more. I'm sure she had miscarriages, but no one talked about it back then.

I was a "breech baby," meaning I came out feet first. Or as my mother said, "You didn't want to come out at all." I also know I caused her a lot of physical pain the day I was born, and the impact of that birth led to various "female problems" as she called them up to the day she died.

Sometimes, we should just thank our moms for going through the agony of giving birth to us. That's especially true to those born years ago when medicine wasn't as advanced as today.

If your mom is alive, ask her to tell you about the day you were born. You could hear an amazing story.

THE WAR, THE MARRIAGE

My mother and father met at tennis courts in what is now Luke Easter Park. My mother told me about my father "being handsome." She was a senior in high school. World War II hung over everything.

"People were getting married fast back then," she said. "You didn't think about it."

My mother wanted out of the house. My father was in the Army. They were married two days after her 18th birthday in the rectory of St. Benedict's Church. My father was Catholic. My mother grew up in a Protestant home, although she rarely went to church as an adult. The religious divide was a factor in our house.

At first, being married was like an adventure to her. The next three years, they lived at one end of the country to the other. They went from Maryland to Washington state to California and places in between—depending upon where my father was stationed.

My brother was born in Santa Barbara, California, in 1945. My father always wished he had stayed in that California town after he was discharged from the service. That was one of his dreams.

A BAD MATCH

My parents barely knew each other when they married. And when they did get to know each other, they realized they didn't like each other much.

Love . . . in their own way.

Like was a different story.

My father wanted a passive Slovak girl who'd stay at home while he made the money working at the old Fisher-Fazio Foods. My mother loved bowling. She went to work at places such as Parmatown and Yorktown Lanes.

Once I was in school, she wanted a career. He wanted her home to put food on the table. She'd yell and argue. He'd shut down and brood. Which led to more yelling, followed by more strained silence.

They almost tormented each other with little things. My father was a "10 minutes early is on time" kind of guy. My mother was 15 minutes late for everything.

"She'll be late for her own funeral," my father often said.

When she had that fatal heart attack, I wished that was true.

Writing this, I realize they probably never talked to each other about their dreams or what they wanted from each other in a marriage.

THEY STUCK IT OUT

They stayed married for 41 years, and I'm grateful for that. They were hard on each other, but great to me. It was painful when they argued. The grudges they held stayed between them. I was Switzerland and they thankfully didn't drag me into their battles.

My mother found a new dream. She helped start a bowling team at Cuyahoga Community College-West. She began teaching bowling classes. This was in the late 1960s. She was the first author in the family, putting together a small self-published textbook for her bowling students.

She knew I wanted to write and was my biggest cheerleader. She helped me find work with a few bowling weekly papers. To her, everything I wrote was wonderful.

She was a hugger, and very enthusiastic about it. She always told me how she loved me.

My father taught me the hard stuff of life. The discipline. The reliability. Be the kind of person others can count upon.

I always knew I had terrific parents. Not perfect. But good enough.

I just wish I had taken time to get to know more of their dreams and their stories.

On Mother's Day, a great gift to some moms would be ask them about theirs—and then thank them for being there for us.

My dad and the purple car

"I got a new car."

I remember my father delivering that news to my mother.

We were living in a small ranch home in Parma, not far from what was the "new" Parmatown shopping center.

My mother took my hand and we went out to look at "the new car."

"Oh, Tom!" she said as if she saw a rhinoceros wallowing in the middle of our driveway.

It indeed was a new car. A huge new car. A huge, purple new car!

This happened about 60 years ago, so I was about 7. I don't remember everything about the car, but it was purple!

It wasn't simply purple. It was very, very purple. It was so purple, you needed sunglasses to look at it very long.

Even my father knew it was ugly.

"I got a good deal on it," he told my mother.

"I bet you did," she said. "Who else would buy it?"

"It runs great," he said.

"It's purple!" she said.

"It's a Chrysler 300," he said. "I always wanted one of these."

"A purple one?" she asked.

"It was on sale," he said.

PLASTIC SEAT COVERINGS

My father opened the car door and the interior was . . . white!

Doesn't everyone dream of a monstrous purple car with a white interior?

My mother started to talk about how the white interior will show all the dirt and stains.

"Look," my father said. "Seat covers came with it."

That's right, the seats were covered with clear plastic. It seemed like a good idea at the time. But as we found out, that plastic would sear the skin off your body in the summertime when the sun beat down through the car windows.

My father again talked about "the great deal" and the "great trade-in" he made with his old car. I think it was a nondescript Dodge. Can't remember much about it. But he did prefer Chrysler/Dodge models to Fords or Chevys. Back then, imported cars were about as rare as a dial telephone is today.

DO YOU HAVE A PURPLE CAR IN YOUR LIFE?

Why am I writing about this in a faith column?

Part of the reason was the memory came back in the last few weeks when reading Christmas recollections from readers. But it's more than that.

Most of us didn't buy a purple car because it seemed like a great idea at the time. It also was so unlike my father, a conservative guy who disdained flashy.

But he liked big cars. He liked making deals and saving money. But he also made a mistake. Is a "good deal" on a dreadful- looking car that was almost embarrassing to drive a good idea?

How many of us have done this in relationships? The person liked to drink when dating, but we thought that will change later. Or the person had anger issues. Or the person was very cheap or perhaps clueless with money?

But the person was available, so maybe the problems will go away—because we want them to.

CAN'T COVER IT UP

Perhaps we try to put the plastic seat covers over it, as my father did with the white interior. We then find out that creates yet another problem.

Obviously, having patience and a willingness to compromise on some things is important to any relationship. But a purple car with a white interior is a purple car with a white interior.

People with major character flaws are people with major character flaws—and it's unfair to expect them to change to please you. If you enter into a serious relationship with them, you are buying them "as is," much like my father did with the purple Chrysler.

Had my father asked my mother (or even a good friend) first before buying the car, he would have saved himself some grief. Before making a major decision, I remind myself to pray about it.

And I also remember to wait, major purchases or commitments don't have to be made immediately.

Too often in life, we allow someone to "sell" us something rather than buying what we really need and know is right for us.

A "good deal" on a "bad product" is not a good deal.

As for my father, I believe he traded in that Chrysler for a Dodge a few years later—much sooner than he usually did with other cars.

Remember: With cars, it's easier to get out of a bad deal. With people, it usually far more painful.

ENERGY VAMPIRES AND OTHER RELATIONSHIPS

Feeling tired? Energy Vampires are exhausting.

"I'm tired."

How often have you said that, or at least thought it?

I'm not talking about the physical fatigue that flattens you after a long day where it seems every bone and muscle ache.

Nor about a day where you spend hours waiting, trying to make your way through the medical system or another bureaucratic obstacle course.

Nor is this about those having physical problems.

Rather, you have a normal day, yet it feels exhausting.

"You're not alone," said Pastor Kevin James of New Community Bible Fellowship in Cleveland Heights. "I've been talking to a lot of people who have been dealing with that tired feeling, along with some anxiety."

DO WE REALLY NEED TO DO MORE?

James said part of the problem is we think we should be doing "more," even if we're not exactly sure what "more" is supposed to be.

The switch to working at home for many people led to unstructured work days. And those who take care of children and/or elderly at home probably are saying, "Welcome to my world, where you never are fully at rest."

Meanwhile, the labor shortage has impacted those on the job. Fewer people are being asked to do more work.

That is true in most retail businesses and elsewhere.

Many of the workers are older. They often make excellent employees because they are reliable, mature and less likely to jump from job to job. But they also have physical limitations. Jobs that didn't seem so demanding in the past are harder now than ever.

"I have mostly an older parish," said Father Tom Haren of St. Monica Church in Garfield Heights. "I'm older, too. You just feel more tired at times."

Haren and James talked about dealing with COVID-19 and all the upheaval in the news. It's like one emotional migraine after another.

"You have to get away from all that," said James, meaning news and politics can wear you down—especially because they usually deal with things we can't control.

THE ENERGY VAMPIRES

A 2018 Healthline story by Kimberly Holland warned of "Energy Vampires," who drain our emotional fuel rather than our blood.

"They feed on your willingness to listen and care for them, leaving you exhausted and overwhelmed," wrote Holland. "They are crafty and may pin problems on someone else in almost every situation. They never accept culpability for their role in any disagreement or issue. You're often left holding the guilt—and possibly the blame."

I also was told the "Energy Vampire" is a character in the comedy show "What We Do in the Shadows." I've never seen it. But like you, I've encountered some real-life Energy Vampires.

"We can't help everyone," said James. "I recently went through this. I was praying about it and realized God didn't expect me to help everyone . . . it was a pride thing. Like I was going to be a spiritual superhero."

THE PROBLEM CAN BE US

Sometimes, the problem is us. We want to please people, so we agree to something knowing it's a bad idea for us. When we become involved, we are resentful.

Many of us need to learn it's easier to start from a "No" and go to a "Yes" than from a "Yes" to a "No." Don't immediately agree to do everything you are asked.

There were times when even Jesus was emotionally squeezed and needed to get away.

He fed 5,000 people in Matthew 14:23, and then, "He sent them away. He went up on the mountain by Himself to pray. When evening came, He was there alone."

The "them" not only were the crowds, but also his immediate circle of friends—his disciples. He had to get away.

"That's why it's so important to be by ourselves and spend time with God," said Haren. "I schedule time each morning."

PRAYING WHILE TIRED

Sometimes, we feel too tired to pray—especially if we consider prayer to be only something formal.

But there are times when simply calling out to God in your weariness is a form of prayer.

Romans 8:26: "The Spirit helps us in our weakness. We do not know what we ought to pray for, but the Spirit himself intercedes for us through wordless groans."

That's how we feel sometimes. We can't form the words, but we know we need a Holy Spirit refill.

Romans 8:27: "And he who searches our hearts knows the mind of the Spirit, because the Spirit intercedes for God's people in accordance with the will of God."

James mentioned the need to be "quiet" before God.

I've done that and fallen asleep, which isn't bad. It's probably what I needed, an answer to the prayer of the weary.

"Something else to do is ask God to show us what is really

going on," said James. "Why are you tired? Pray for clarity. Then when you hear something, pray for the courage to act upon it if you really want to change."

What does a woman want? Ask her.

I was talking to someone who mentioned he was recently married.

I congratulated him and mentioned Roberta and I had our 44th anniversary.

"Really?" he said. "How did you do it?"

"Do you really want to know?" I asked.

He did. I opened with this story.

In early September, my wife and I went away for a few days to celebrate her birthday and our anniversary. (BTW: We've been married 44 years, but she's only 31. That's good math for guys to keep in mind.)

Anyway, we were hiking part of the Buckeye Trail in a very rural part of southern Ohio. We talked a little about our marriage, how we've known each other for 47 years.

"Is there anything I can do better?" I asked.

She was quiet.

"I'm serious," I said. "I want to know. I promise, I'll listen."

It's a bit scary to ask a question like that, and even harder to promise not to immediately become defensive.

"I wish you'd listen to me more," she said. "There are times when I start to tell you something, and I can tell you aren't interested. Sometimes, I figure I'll just shut up and tell God about it later."

It stung, because it's true. I zone out at times when she is telling me something about the church choir or people we know.

LOOK AT ME!

A little background: Roberta rarely complains. If the Browns had scouted and drafted as well as I did with Roberta when they were looking for a quarterback, they'd have been playing for the Super Bowl every year.

Making the situation even more pronounced, I had recently listened to a message by Pastor Rick Warren. The author of "The Purpose Driven Life" stopped in the middle of a sermon on another topic and said, "Guys, when your wife or someone is talking to you . . . LOOK AT HER!"

Ouch.

After Roberta brought up the point about listening, I was quiet. I wanted to tell her about all the times I did listen, but it would just shut her down.

Then I said some painful but powerful words, "You're right. I will do better. I promise."

I've been working on it the last few weeks. Not only make eye contact, but ask questions. Say things like. "Tell me more . . ." or "How did that make you feel?"

Be the biggest fan of your spouse/friend. Remember what you did when you first met and were very interested in each other.

FRIENDSHIP IS ABOUT SOMETHING

I asked her for some thoughts about relationships. It doesn't just apply to marriage. Her thoughts on listening apply to everyone.

One of the things on her list is "Find something to do with each other—walking, hiking, sports, plays."

Or as C.S. Lewis wrote in his book *The Four Loves*: "Friendship has to be about something, even if it were enthusiasm for dominoes or white mice."

I knew almost zero about the outdoors and hiking when I met Roberta. She loves those things. We dated for 3½ years. She knew little about pro sports but liked to play basketball. She was on the first women's team in Hiram College history.

She picked up on sports with me. I learned to love the outdoors with her. Both of us love reading and she was editing my writing even before we were married. Forty-seven years, she's still doing it—God love her!

The key is to continue to make time to do the things that first brought you together. She likes to dine out, so we make a date a few times a month. The place doesn't have to be expensive. It's about making time for each other.

You don't have to do everything together. When it comes to singing, the best I can do is what the Bible calls "make a joyful noise" in Psalm 100. Roberta took eight years of classical voice lessons. It shows.

THE POWER OF TOUCH

On her list, Roberta wrote: "Most men need sex to feel loved and build intimacy with their wives. Women need to be told they are loved often. They need hugs that don't lead to sex."

This is something we became very intentional about several years ago—hugs and quick kisses that are just that, a way to touch that wasn't about sex. Hold each other's hands.

One of our favorite marriage books is *The Five Love Languages* by Gary Chapman. We've read it out loud together, bought lots of copies to give to friends—not just married couples.

Our love languages are "Quality Time" and "Physical Touch." For others, it's things like gifts, acts of service and words of affirmation.

Entire books are written on this subject, so a lot is left out in this story. But here are a few quick thoughts:

1. No negative name-calling. Never. Even if the person pretends it doesn't hurt, it probably does.

2. Never criticize your spouse to others, unless it's a counseling situation. And never criticize a friend/spouse in front of other people, even if you think it's funny.

3. If you're married, never mention the word divorce. Ruth (wife of Billy) Graham was once asked if she ever considered

divorcing her husband. "Divorce? No!" she asked. "But murder
. . . Yes!" Then she laughed.

4. That said, Roberta and I have lots of friends and family
members who have been divorced—many for good reasons. So
this is not to beat up on people who have endured a divorce. But
it is to say don't go into a marriage thinking, "Well, if it goes bad,
I can always get divorced."

5. Not only pray for each other, pray together. It can be strange
and awkward at first. But remember, praying is talking with God.
We pray each morning and most nights. Doesn't have to be long,
but it keeps you together.

How to 'make up' for lost time in a relationship

"I wish we could just have a normal relationship."

Linda (not her real name) said this to me when talking about how her son suddenly has come back into her life. She was hit hard with an illness, spent a few weeks in the hospital.

The son would make contact perhaps a few times a year, nothing very deep.

"But since I got sick, he wants to come in and run everything," she said.

He's not even asking her what she wants him to do, he wants to "take over and tell me what to do."

"Do you think he's trying to make up for lost time?" I asked.

"What do you mean?" Linda asked.

"Maybe he knows that he should have been more involved in your life," I said. "Now that you're older and had this health scare, he feels guilty. Like he's trying to make up for lost time."

"That could be it," she said. "But this isn't the right way to do it. I feel like he's bossing me around and making me a nervous wreck."

I thought about that for a moment.

"The problem with trying to make up for lost time is you can't," I said. "It leads to overcompensating, trying to do now—all at once—what should have been done for years."

That's when Linda mentioned her heart aching for a "normal relationship."

WHAT SHOULD BE DONE?

If you want to "make up" for time lost and mistakes made, remember you don't make the rules.

That's the problem with her son's approach. He wants to return to his mother's life by "fixing her." And he wants to do it his way.

It's a temptation.

We say things like, "OK, how about I write a check for . . ."

Or, "How about I buy you . . ."

Or as Linda discovered, her son thought the best thing was for him to rearrange her life.

"I just wish he'd ask me what I want him to do," she said.

Yes, asking would be good.

But even better would be starting with an apology.

How do you make up for "lost time"? You begin by admitting time was lost—and it was your fault.

That's not easy. It's going to take prayer. It will require what the Bible calls a humble and contrite heart (Psalm 51:17).

Or Ephesians 4:2: "With all humility and gentleness, with patience, bearing with one another in love."

WHO DEFINES THE RELATIONSHIP?

The person who has been hurt will require us to approach them with "humility, patience and gentleness."

If we are primarily responsible for the fracture in the relationship, we should first apologize. Then we need to ask, "How do you want to go from here? What kind of relationship would you like?"

While Linda's situation is with a son, it often is the other way. Parents divorce. Or they leave. And suddenly they want to return to the lives of their children.

The people left behind have been hurt. It would be natural for them to be suspicious. Trust was broken.

WHAT COMES NEXT?

In some cases, it makes sense not to allow a dangerous person back into your life. Many people confuse "forgiveness" with "reconciliation."

Those are two steps.

Pastor Rick Warren (author of *The Purpose Driven Life*) defines forgiveness as giving up the "right to get even." It means not obsessing on the hurts or letting them rule your emotional life.

The next step is restoring the relationship. OK, what will the relationship be—if there will even be one—going forward? The person who was hurt and left behind has the right to set up the boundaries.

That often means going slowly. It also means stop blaming and rehashing the old history that tends to only lead everyone in a circle of frustration.

Remember, lost time is lost. We can't "make up" for it. But we can start to do things the right way, do them slowly and most of all, do them with a humble heart.

Haunted by the 'What Ifs?'

I call them "phony fears."

They are things we worry about that:

A. Never happened.

B. We can't control.

For example, I was worried about my 95-year-old "Mom," Melva Hardison, taking the COVID-19 vaccine. Along with other family members, we urged her to get the shots. The virus is brutal on the elderly.

We also couldn't visit her until we all were vaccinated.

Well, she took the shots. Had zero side effects. Of course there were risks with or without the shot, but the odds of staying well were better for her after being vaccinated.

But here's another point: My worrying had no impact on how she handled the shot. Pray and wait was the best formula.

Instead, I had a few hours of being haunted by the "What Ifs?"

"The news can cause a lot of that," said Bishop Joey Johnson of Akron's House of the Lord. "Fear of the virus. Fear of the vaccine. Fear of everything from climate change to social unrest to the economy."

It seems to never end, especially if we don't turn off the news.

"When we really start to worry, we feel as if the thing is actually happening to us . . . even though it's not," said Johnson.

WHAT ARE YOU WORRIED ABOUT?

Here are some other examples readers posted on my Facebook page:

"I worry about my grandson bailing on his responsibility. He hasn't so far."

"As a believer, I know nothing can compare with being with Jesus. But I worry what will happen to my family after I die. I worry if I'll see my daughter get married and have grandchildren."

"I worried about lines at gas stations. So far, no lines in Ohio."

"When my daughter was little, I dreamed she was lost in a crowd. She's 14 now. We still hold hands in a crowd. I fear for her safety because it's a tough world out there."

"I worried there wouldn't be a vaccine. Now I worry not enough people will take it."

"My daughter had a TBI (Traumatic Brain Injury) at 5. She has a high IQ, but some issues that come with TBI . . . God finds a way. My little girl just completed her first year of art college. I tell parents so much of what we worry about is truly unimportant."

"In 2017, I found out I had cancer. It went away with treatment, then came back in 2018. Last week, I got my 66th chemo treatment since May 2018. My tests are good, but I still need chemo. I don't worry nearly as much as I used to . . . Maybe a little about the Tribe not hitting."

THE SPIRITUAL BATTLE

Over and over again, we hear how a crisis forces us to "put things in perspective." The "little things" really are "little things" when we are faced with a medical problem or how to help an elderly relative.

Bishop Johnson remembered going to a church as a child where occasionally someone "prophesied" over another person with grim predictions of death or doom.

"Some churches focus so much on the 'end times,' they miss the love and grace of God to get us through today," he said. "Feeling fear is real, even if the fear isn't founded in reality."

Johnson mentioned Jesus asking, "Can any one of you by worrying add a single hour to your life?" (Matthew 6:27).

He also mentioned St. Paul writing: "Do not be anxious about anything, but in everything by prayer and petition and with thanks present your requests to God." (Philippians 4:6).

"Everything" means our fears and worries. Admit them to a few close friends. Ask them to pray with you and for you.

WISDOM FROM READERS

"I try not to worry about things I cannot control . . . which is most things."

"I worried about many things in my life and it usually was a precious waste of time."

"Prayer is my rock. A friend once told me that any day we are living above the roses is a good day."

"I've found most of the things I worry about are usually not the things that happen."

"Worry is a wasted emotion. It takes away logical thinking about how to resolve the crisis that does arise. We need a calm demeanor in emergencies to think clearly without losing focus."

ARE YOU A WORRIER?

Some people take pride in being a worrier, as if it makes them more caring than others. They look for things to worry about.

They might even become angry when others aren't as worried or anxious about the same things they are feeling.

This can be very destructive to those around the chronic/angry worrier. Who wants to be around that hyper-anxious person for a long period of time?

"We have to be humble enough to admit we are not God, we can't fix everything," said Johnson. "When we keep worrying about what happened in the past or what will happen in the future, we lose the present."

Obviously, all the challenges life brings require some preparation.

"But when we worry so much, we forget God wants to be with us today," said Johnson. "That's the first step in dealing with worry: Going to God right now about it."

People Pleasers: Before you say 'Yes,' consider this

A few months before Mary (not her real name) was to be married, she knew it was a bad idea. She was afraid to tell anyone. But about a week before the wedding, she opened up to her parents.

They also had doubts about the person she was marrying.

"Call it off," they said. "We'll support you."

"What will other people think?" she asked. "We made all these plans."

"Don't worry about it," they said.

"If I don't marry him, then no one will want me," she said.

The discussion went on for a long time. She later talked to her boyfriend.

"They went through with the wedding," said Father John Thomas Lane of St. Paschal Baylon Catholic Church in Highland Heights.

Lane didn't officiate this wedding. It was a story told to him by a friend.

He also has heard other versions of it: People getting married and making other life-changing decisions because they were more worried about the opinion of others than the right thing to do.

The woman ended up in a messy marriage with lots of heartbreak and eventually, a painful divorce.

WHAT HAPPENS WHEN WE SAY 'YES'

I was sure business writer Stephen Covey (*The 7 Habits of*

Highly Effective People) said: "Whenever you say yes to something, you say no to something else."

I couldn't find the source of that exact quote.

Covey did write: "You have to decide what your highest priorities are and have the courage—pleasantly, smilingly, nonapologetically—to say 'no' to other things. And the way you do that is by having a bigger 'yes' burning inside. The enemy of the 'best' is often the 'good.' "

That led to another story from Lane.

He didn't begin college with being a priest in mind. He was a talented musician and that was his major. When he graduated, he had three job offers to teach music.

Lane also had friends and family members encouraging him to go to New York: "Give Broadway a shot. You'll always regret it if you don't try."

But Lane had clearly experienced the pull of God on his life. If he walked away from music, he knew some people close to him would believe he was "wasting his talent."

"There are times when no matter what you do, you will make some people unhappy," said Lane. "Some people wanted me to be a priest, even more wanted me to have a career in music."

He followed both his heart and God's leading and became a priest. That was 30 years ago.

"I've never regretted it," he said.

EVERYDAY DECISIONS

Although the first two stories are about life-changing decisions, we say "yes" and "no" to "smaller things" almost every day.

Some of us would rather gargle with Drano and rusty nails than say "no" to someone wanting a favor—even though we know it's a bad idea.

Making it worse, we take on the task and feel resentful inside. We think about something else we could be doing—maybe should be doing. We are angry at the person who asked, as if they forced us to do it.

But whose fault is it? Who are we really trying to please?

There are times when we need to turn down something because we are emotionally and/or physically drained. Staying home is the right move to recharge, even if the alternative seems more attractive when it arises.

Matthew 14:23: "After Jesus had dismissed the crowd, he went up on a mountainside by himself to pray. Later that night, he was there alone."

There are times when we need to be alone. To think. To pray. To rest.

Don't expect those asking you for a favor to understand. Don't feel the need to explain.

Just say, "Sorry, I have another commitment."

WHAT DOES COME FIRST?

It can be picking your child's T-ball game or school play over yet another business meeting, as a high-level executive recently told me that he forced himself to do.

"I say I put family first," he said. "It was time for me to show it. And I knew, there were meetings coming soon. I'll be there for them. But for now, I had to be there for the kids."

It was a struggle, but he knew by saying "No" to the meeting he also was saying "Yes" to his family.

Women have often told me how they feel "like I have to be in two places at once." That's true. But it's also true that can't happen.

"If the Devil can't make you sin, he'll make you busy" is a quote attributed to several different people.

It's partly correct. We actually make ourselves busy based on what we say "Yes" to when asked.

CAN YOU DO ME A FAVOR?

When someone says, "Can you do me a favor," never say "Yes."

I always ask, "What is the favor?"

To some, that might seem impolite, but it's common sense. Who knows what the person wants? The moment you agree, then you are on the defensive of trying to get out of something you never knew was coming.

I know a salesman who told me, "If you want someone to do what you want, ask them to 'help' you. Most people want to help. It makes them feel good."

How many people—especially young people—have followed friends into reckless choices? They knew it was wrong, but wanted to be accepted.

It's why we need to approach this on a spiritual level. God does not want us to take on every task available to us.

Consider John 6:15: "Jesus, knowing that they intended to come and make him king by force, withdrew again to a mountain by himself."

Jesus turned down what would be considered an earthly promotion for a higher calling. That's true for us when we try to convince someone to like us by doing what they want—even if it's not a good idea.

Tired of trying to fix someone else's life? Here's how to stop.

"I've tried everything."

Many times, I've heard those words from people.

They've tried to get their kid off drugs. In and out of treatment centers, thousands of dollars spent.

They've tried to help a friend get and keep a job. But he keeps getting fired or quitting.

They have had serious talks with someone close to them about seeking counseling for their temper or wild personality swings.

And what changes? Usually, not much.

"It's the myth of thinking we're somehow in control of another's life," said Father Walt Jenne, who is semi-retired but still ministering four days a week at St. Helen Catholic Church in Newbury.

I saw this headline on a column by Amy Dickinson: "Ask Amy: How do I make my sister see she is the problem, and to stop blaming other people for life's woes?"

I wanted to scream, "Hey, sister . . . YOU CAN'T!" Often, the last person who wants to hear your advice is a sibling.

DO YOU WANT TO GET WELL?

As a priest, Jenne is often asked, "Please talk to my son; I don't know what to do with him."

Jenne usually agrees to a meeting, assuming the person is willing to talk to him. Sometimes, they won't even do that.

"I can't change them and you can't change them," Jenne will

tell the parent. "The older I get, the more I realize how powerless I am in these situations. God has to be involved."

Jenne has friends who are in Alcoholics Anonymous. He's learned a lot from that program.

"I've gone on vacations with them and attended their meetings," he said. "You listen to the stories. You realize how the change didn't come until they were ready to do it. Then they admitted how they needed God to take over."

No outside person alone convinced them to stop drinking or getting high.

In John, chapter 5, Jesus encounters a man who has been "an invalid for 38 years. When Jesus saw him lying there and learned that he had been in this condition for a long time, he asked him, 'Do you want to get well?' "

Why ask that question?

Because being healed—or becoming sober, or more responsible—will mean a major life alteration. That scares some people.

That's why it appears we want them to change more than they do. Down deep, they really don't want to get well.

WHAT ABOUT ME?

I've known some people obsessed with trying to fix a certain person.

"Some of it is because they are embarrassed by the conduct of the person," said Jenne. "You want them to change because they are making you or your family look bad to others."

All of us have times when we think, "If only that person would listen to me, things would be so much better."

We indeed might be giving them good advice. But also telling others what to do feeds part of our ego.

"(We want them to know) they are wrong," wrote Beverly Flaxington in Psychology Today. "Not only are they wrong, but they are in need of your fixing. Of course . . . the more you try and correct someone else's behavior, the less likely they are to listen to you and make the shifts."

Many of us have been hurt by the actions of people close to us. We can't believe some of their ridiculous decisions. Parents wonder: "How can my child act like this? She didn't learn that at home!"

In the meantime, our approach isn't working.

"You might want the person to admit to wrongdoing," wrote Flaxington. "They need to prove you right and say so."

That could be the last thing that person will do, even if they know you are right. Too much family mess is involved.

WHAT TO DO?

"When you give advice or offer help, you can't make it personal," said Jenne. "And that's hard."

We need to ask ourselves this question: Why am I so invested in this troubled person?

And these questions: Does my being involved with this troubled person negatively impact my other relationships? Are they sick of hearing me talk about the person over and over?

A woman once told me, "A mother can only be as happy as how her most troubled child is doing."

The mother didn't mean it as selfish, but it comes across that way. Why should her other kids have to suffer her moods because their sibling is causing trouble?

Trying to fix people can lead to being fixated on the wrong people—and ignoring others who need us. Just a fraction of attention given to the kid with a problem would be greatly appreciated by the others in the family.

Why become an emotional hostage to another's moods and decisions? Jenne talked about the need to "pray for the person, then trust God to work on them."

Sure, we can give advice. We can even plead and pray with the person. But understand how damaging it can be if we take the rejection very personally.

I like this verse: Philippians 4:8: "Finally, brothers and sisters, whatever is true, whatever is noble, whatever is right, whatever is pure, whatever is lovely, whatever is admirable—if anything is excellent or praiseworthy—think about such things."

There often is so much good around us, if only we'd stop and notice it—and praise those who are doing the right things.

Pets can help us cope

My wife and I were walking through a park recently when a woman came by with her big, white fluffy dog.

"His name is Arthur," she said.

"What kind of a dog is he?" I asked.

"I don't know," she said. "Just a big mutt. But he is the best 50 bucks that I ever spent."

She has had Arthur for 13 years, and it was easy to see that they have been through a lot together.

My friend Gloria had a dog named Spice for 18 years. The collie mix was like her big brother. He was her bodyguard and made this single woman feel safe.

The mother of a friend recently had a major stroke. My friend has been spending hours and hours at a hospital, about an hour from her home. She has been staying at her mother's house during this ordeal.

Because I dealt with my father's stroke in the 1990s, we have been talking often. My wife and I made the hour drive to the hospital, talked and prayed with her and her mother.

At one point, completely exhausted, she said, "I miss my cats."

She lives alone—well, along with her three cats. She hasn't seen them for days. A friend was feeding and checking on them while she was at her mother's bedside.

"Go see the brats," I said. "OK, I mean the cats."

It's one of those inside jokes that is funny only to those involved.

One of the cats is Casper—he's white and he's almost deaf. And he also is one of the friendliest cats that I've ever met.

So what's the point about a discussion of dogs and cats in a column called Faith & You?

It's that one of God's great gifts to many of us are our pets. In times of stress, they are smart enough to stick by us—but not say a word.

There is a biblical character named Job who endures all types of disasters and heartbreak.

He has three friends who hear about Job's trials, and when they show up, "They sat on the ground with him for seven days and seven nights. No one said a word to him, because they saw how great his suffering was."

Later, they begin to talk to Job, and lots of problems arise. Boy, have I fallen into that trap!

But when they were silent, it gave Job comfort.

Maybe that's why my wife and others have said they find it easier to get along with animals than people.

A good pet can sense when we are distressed, and often comes even closer to us—yet offers no advice, delivers no lectures.

Chapter 3 of the book of Daniel is about three men thrown into a "fiery furnace" because they wouldn't bow down and worship the king.

But when the king looks into the furnace, the three men aren't burning, and there is a fourth man walking with them.

Biblical scholars love to debate if the fourth man was an angel (which the Bible indicates) or something else. But the fourth man never speaks, he is just with the other three. When they come out of the furnace, the fourth man is not with them.

A friend told me, "We all need a furnace friend, someone who can walk with us when it gets hot and scary."

Sometimes, our pets are "furnace friends," and they can teach us a lot about how we can be there for others.

SO THIS IS CHRISTMAS

Christmas with my father at the Waffle House

Once in a while, someone asks me about "The Waffle House story." It's something I've written about a few times in different ways, the last being in 2011.

It's a Christmas story.

It's a father/son story.

It's a bit of a misfit story.

And yes, it's a Waffle House story.

There's something about a Waffle House that I've loved from the moment I first walked through the doors. That was in North Carolina when I was a rookie reporter at the Greensboro News-Record in 1977. I worked the late afternoon shift, which ended around 1 a.m.

Where do you go to eat at 1 a.m. in Greensboro, I wondered.

"The Waffle House," my friend Bob Bevan said. "It's always open."

Back then, the Waffle House was mostly in the South. Now it's almost everywhere, nearly 2,000 locations.

And yes, it's always open, 365 days, 24/7.

That's an important part of this story.

PICTURES ON THE MENU

Former Tribe shortstop Omar Vizquel once told me about his first year in pro baseball. He was a 17-year-old from Venezuela who signed with the Seattle Mariners and was assigned to play in Butte, Montana.

He found the Waffle House. There was cheap food and lots of it.

"The menu also had pictures of food," said Vizquel. "I was in Montana. I couldn't speak a word of English. But I could point to the pictures on the menu when I ordered. I also could learn the names of food that way."

That conversation with Vizquel was from the middle 1990s. That was when my father was still living in Sarasota, Florida. He suffered a major stroke in 1993. We had home health care helping to take care of him. My brother, Tom, lived nearby. I went to Sarasota for at least several days every month during the last four years of his life.

I had forgotten that story from Vizquel until I began to write about the Waffle House this week.

The pictures on the menu . . .

That was important to my father.

Not only had the stroke paralyzed his right side and taken away his speech, it also robbed him of the ability to read. But at the Waffle House, he could look at the menu and point at what he wanted—instead of having me order for him when we went to other restaurants.

When you go to the Waffle House, you know what to expect. It's about breakfasts. It's about meat, potatoes and grease on the grill. It's about the sound of sizzling bacon and waitresses yelling out orders.

It's about waffles. It's about sitting at the counter or in a small booth, watching people cook your food.

WHEN YOU HAVE NOWHERE ELSE TO GO

One Christmas, I was with Dad in Sarasota. He wanted to go out to eat. But where?

Waffle House. That was our first trip together to the Waffle House.

I remember a rough-looking guy with jail tattoos behind the grill. I remember a waitress who looked very tired, worn down by life.

I remember a few other solitary souls scattered about. It was near a hospital and it was easy to imagine some of the lonely people there thinking about someone they've just visited, someone in very bad shape.

And I remember how the waitress smiled when I rolled my father into the place in his wheelchair. I remember the cook hearing the order from the waitress, looking up at my dad and saying, "Comin' right up!"

I remember my dad laughing.

I remember some of folks at the counter, saying "hello," others nodding in our direction.

The Waffle House Christmas Night Fraternity.

THE FIRST CHRISTMAS

It's a good guess that if there was a Waffle House in Bethlehem more than 2,000 years ago, Joseph might have taken his bride, Mary, there to eat.

They had traveled more than 70 miles on foot (or perhaps on a donkey) from their home in Nazareth to Bethlehem to register for a census and pay taxes. The Gospel writer Luke describes how Joseph and about-to-give-birth Mary ended up in what basically was a barn with animals.

"She brought forth her firstborn son, and wrapped him in swaddling clothes. She laid him in a manger; because there was no room for them in the inn." (Luke 2:7)

Other versions say, "because there was no guest room." I'll let the scholars battle that out.

The point is, the couple had nowhere else to go. Furthermore, the first visitors to see Jesus were shepherds, the kind of guys who would feel very comfortable at the Waffle House late at night.

To Christians, this is the story of how the Son of God was born. The Savior of the World welcomed mostly by those who felt like misfits, and those later became the people He treasured.

People like my father, myself and the rest of us at Waffle House on Christmas night.

Remember when there was no room at the inn in your life?

The year was 1979, and I had just been hired as the new baseball writer for the Baltimore Evening Sun, covering the Orioles.

It was a shock.

Ten days earlier, I was working in Savannah, Georgia. I had covered the Class AA Braves farm team. I was less than two full years out of Cleveland State.

But suddenly, the Evening Sun needed someone (young and cheap) to cover the Orioles. It's a long, improbable story that led to me being hired. And being told to get to spring training in Miami. . .yesterday.

NO VACANCY

My wife, Roberta, and I had driven from Savannah to Baltimore for the interview. They offered me the job on the spot. We then drove back to Savannah, threw some things in the car—and started to drive to Miami.

Somewhere in Northern Florida, both of us were exhausted. We couldn't find a hotel (this was tourist season). We hadn't thought to make a reservation.

As it said in Luke chapter 2:7: "There was no room for them in the inn."

We found a campground. It had a "No Vacancy" sign. A gate locked the entrance. But there was a place to pull off the road. We did and slept for a few hours in our bucket of bolts, an old Dodge Dart.

I remember feeling like a failure because of my lack of planning. We were sweaty, dirty, hungry, frazzled, and my wife of 18 months had to wonder, "Just who did I marry?"

After 46 years together, Roberta should get the MVW award: Most Valuable Wife!

Looking back, there was no need to rush to Miami in a frenzy, but I was excited and afraid at the same time. I wanted to get to work in Miami before the Sun realized they'd hired a raw rookie and changed their minds.

Roberta sensed my feelings and insecurity. She didn't complain even though she had to be more than a little overwhelmed and frustrated by everything happening so fast.

NO ROOM AT THE INN

I've read the account of the birth of Jesus at least 100 times.

Mary is ready to give birth. Her husband (Joseph) has to travel 70 miles from their hometown of Nazareth to Bethlehem to register for a Roman census. The real reason was the Romans wanted to count everyone to collect taxes.

Unlike our trip from Savannah to Miami, Mary and Joseph didn't have a car. Seventy miles on foot (or even on the back of a donkey for Mary) was no joy ride.

Joseph had relatives in Bethlehem, the city of David. It's why he had to report there. But many scholars believe "no room in the inn" actually means none of the relatives were able (or willing) to make room for Joseph and his new wife.

BORN IN A BARN?

Someone set them up in a stable, and that's where Jesus was born.

There had to be straw and rodents and animals and smells and dirt—nothing like the neat and beautiful manger scene we often find with various Christmas decorations.

Jesus was born into a chaotic world where the Romans were oppressing his Jewish people. And he was born to young, frightened parents who had to feel rejected when they ended up in a barn.

Who were the first visitors?

Shepherds, who had been spending day and night with their sheep on a nearby hillside. They probably smelled like they slept outside. In many temples, they had to watch the services from the courtyard because they were deemed too low-class to be with the regular religious folk.

This story was far more gritty than pretty.

And Mary and Joseph had to wonder, "This is God's plan for our lives? Really?"

CHRISTMAS & REJECTION & HOPE

At the very least, the first Christmas was haunted by poor preparation, at least in human terms. God's plans don't always match ours.

They also had to feel rejected. Mary probably wondered why Joseph's relatives weren't more helpful. And Joseph had to feel somewhat like I did in that campground on the road to Miami.

Jesus was born into Family Mess, as called by Bishop Joey Johnson of Akron's House of the Lord.

And 2,000 years later, most of us have to deal with Family Mess—especially during the holidays. Many of us have to pray for God's wisdom and patience as we deal with the people in our lives.

That's especially true in 2020, when it seems nothing has any chance of going as planned with all the restrictions on family gatherings and travel.

And we need to remember God doesn't expect perfection from us.

One of my favorite verses is John 3:17: "God did not send his Son into the world to condemn the world, but to save the world through Him."

There are many more major theological themes from the birth of Jesus that can have lifelong implications.

But in the middle of so many things going wrong, we should be reminded not to be defined by those who reject us.

Just as God called the shepherds to be the first to see Jesus, he does the same for us—even if there are times when we don't feel worthy.

Ghosts of Christmas past and hoping for a joyous present

The odor of garlic coming from the kitchen.

The warm smell of fresh chocolate chip cookies giving your nose a warm hug.

The visitor who comes with a box from Hough Bakery. It's tied closed with a string. Cupcakes inside.

The uncle who drinks too much, talks too loud and everyone tries to ignore.

The aunt who wants to tell everyone, "Eat . . . EAT . . . EAT!" On top of that, she has hearing problems and keeps screaming, "HUH?" She also worked forever at May Company because she loved getting the employee "10% discount."

The grandfather who loves pierogies, especially those with prunes to help with his bowels.

WHEN THE WAR WAS THE WAR

There is another uncle who rarely comes to the Christmas dinners. Once, he did. I heard he had been at Pearl Harbor when the bombs were falling, and I asked him about it.

"It was Sunday morning," the uncle said. "I was coming out of church. All hell broke loose. We hid under the table for a few minutes until we figured out what was going on."

Then he said no more. World War II wasn't that long ago back then. It was simply known as "The War."

The woman cooking in the kitchen tells you again to check "the milk box." The milk man was supposed to deliver on Christmas Eve in time for the company to arrive.

Maybe this comes with age. Maybe it's part phony nostalgia. Maybe it's a wish for a time that is far less complicated than today.

NOTICE HOW GIFTS RECEDE FROM MEMORY

Perhaps you are different. Perhaps much of your Christmas revolved around gifts, and you remember many you received.

I don't.

I remember family, good and bad.

I grew up in a Slovak household. For my grandparents on both sides, English was a second language.

The television was black and white, three channels. Two newspapers came to the house, the *Plain Dealer* and the old *Cleveland Press*.

Want to know the weather report? Check the weather report at 6 or 11 p.m. on TV. Or maybe see what "the paper" had to say. If it's December, you'd better make sure you have "snow tires" on your car.

There were arguments in my house about what relatives would host the supper on Christmas Eve, or the late-afternoon get-together on Christmas Day.

There also were annual verbal fights between my parents. That happens when the father thinks being on time is at least 10 minutes early—and the mother figures it's no problem being 15 to 30 minutes late.

I remember being allowed to stay up late on Christmas Eve. That's because we went to Midnight Mass. That was so long ago, it was in Latin. Felt like an eternity for a little kid thinking about what Santa would leave under the tree on Christmas morning.

YES, GOD WAS THERE

In my family, God wasn't talked about much. There was a quick prayer before we ate. Church on Sunday was mandatory. My father would say: "You put money in the (collection) basket. Don't worry, you always get it back."

Believe me, that tough warehouse man was not into the prosperity gospel. He simply believed in doing what was right—the idea of reaping and sowing.

God was there because otherwise, some of these people probably would have killed each other—or at least stopped talking for decades.

Instead, they kept getting together. The men played lots of cards—pinochle. The women went into the kitchen to talk. I do recall something about saving "S&H Green Stamps" and trading them in for stuff.

As for the kids, I don't remember what we did. But I do know this: We didn't stare at our cellphones.

The only phone was bolted to the wall—and it was a party line. Christmas . . .

I remember someone once telling me about how it is to get older: "One day, it's Christmas," he said. "And the next day, it's another Christmas. It's like that year after year."

So it is . . .

Merry Christmas, everyone.

CAN I FORGIVE
MYSELF?

God may have forgiven her, but she still can't forgive herself

"I keep looking back at my life and wondering what I did wrong."

Kay (not her real name) mentioned that to me.

She had been telling me about her recent health issues, a trip to the hospital when Crohn's disease acted up. She also had other internal problems.

She has dealt with these problems for decades.

"When I was younger, I slept with a couple of married guys," she said. "A long time ago, I did some cocaine."

Her voice trailed off.

It's been many years since she slept with married guys. It was a long time ago when she used drugs.

But sometimes when we're under physical and emotional stress, we circle back to what we did wrong years ago.

So much of life is a spiritual battle.

It's why a broken heart seems to take so much longer to heal than a broken arm or leg.

I began to talk to Kay about forgiveness. She believes in God. On one level, she believes God has forgiven her. But she finds it hard to forgive herself.

One of my favorite Bible verses is 2 Corinthians 5:17: "If anyone is in Christ, that person is a new creation. The old has gone, the new is here."

I mentioned that to her.

She DID those things . . . past tense.

She is NOT those things today. God is not punishing her through her health problems. We talked quite a while about that . . . who she was vs. who she is today.

And she had changed . . . for the better.

BEING STUCK

For several weeks, I've been teaching a series to the guys at Summit County Jail about "Being Stuck."

We started with Cain and Abel, how Cain was stuck on jealousy and bitterness toward his brother.

Fact: At some point, everyone is stuck on something.

When I said that, one of the men mentioned having a broken heart about not being able to have a last conversation with his mother before she died.

Many of us carry something like that around.

"I should have been there," we say.

Maybe we should have been there.

A former good friend from high school reached out to me a few years ago. We hadn't talked for a long time. I had his number. I kept it by the phone. Several months went by.

Then I received word that he had suddenly died.

I looked at the number, a few tears in my eyes.

I should have called . . . but didn't.

When those feelings of regret come, I have to battle them on a spiritual level.

OUR REAL ENEMY

I believe we have a spiritual enemy. The Bible calls it Satan.

Isn't it easy to turn a two-minute conversation into a two-hour reality show in our heads?

We go over . . .

And over . . .

And over . . .

The same stuff, and often it's just stupid stuff. Or it's stuff we can't fix . . . like missing a chance at a last conversation.

There are times when I stop and pray, "Lord, I'm getting stuck on stupid . . . I need you to free me."

Sometimes, I hear, "Get off yourself and go to work."

That can be anything from my job to working out to calling or visiting someone.

GETTING FREE

There are people who don't want to hear about spiritual battles or anything that hints at the biblical view of Satan.

But there are so many reasons people who are stuck begin to self-medicate. We can do it with everything from alcohol to drugs to pornography to gambling to obsessively watching certain shows for hours at a time.

We sense we are in a battle and we want relief. But we don't want to face the real enemy.

A person can pray alone. A person can also reach out to someone to pray together.

At church, some people stick around after the service to pray . . . but probably not as many as should, given the battles we face.

When someone tells you about a problem, say, "Let's pray about it right now."

The prayer can be quick and quiet, especially in a public place. But do it.

One of the most dangerous ways to stay stuck is to never tell anyone about it.

Obviously, you need to be careful about some subjects.

But Kay opening up about her health issues and doubts led to a discussion and a quick prayer that did bring her some relief.

It's also why the proper type of counseling can help. I also think the Catholic sacrament of confession is very valuable to some people.

We all get stuck on something, sometimes.

Now we need to know we can't always face it alone.

Regrets are powerful, but so is forgiveness

"It is easier to say 'my tooth is aching' than to say 'My heart is broken.'"

C.S. Lewis wrote that in his book *The Problem of Pain*.

When I have spoken in jails and elsewhere, I've often asked, "Do we learn more from pleasure or pain?"

The answer comes back quickly—pain.

I wrote about the March 10, 2021 death of Joe Tait, the Cavs' broadcaster and one of my closest friends. Joe was in a lot of pain as he dealt with bladder and colon cancer, a major blood clot in his leg and kidney failure. He'd occasionally joke how he wondered what malady "would get me first."

Most people don't die of one thing unless there is an accident or tragedy. It's a combination. Just as most of us don't really lose our temper over one comment or incident. It's a product of what happened during the day.

"Death by a thousand paper cuts," is a phrase that comes to mind.

Or a thousand frustrations, even if it's a few that repeat over and over.

THE REAL PAIN

When Joe and I talked about death, life and time running out, he insisted more than once, "I'm not afraid to die."

It wasn't a defiant statement. It wasn't designed to sound spiritual because Joe said he wasn't sure about God or an afterlife. It was almost as if he was reading the final score of a Cavs game as he was signing off his broadcast.

But part of what ached his heart was leaving behind his wife, Jean. She had been in an Alzheimer's unit for more than five years. It's been longer than that since she called him by name.

"Sometimes, she'd say 'husband,'" said Joe. "But mostly, I was some guy who showed up every day at dinner time to help feed her."

But even that was taken away when COVID-19 hit and visitors were kept out of extended senior living facilities. Most of us believe Joe kept Jean in his home for a few years longer than it was wise. He knew she was slipping away mentally and feared it would be worse if he wasn't always there for her.

Joe was very thankful for his family and good friends. But there are always things we wish we hadn't done or said. We talked about that in our lives. One of the subjects was how many parents beat themselves up emotionally for not always having "been there" for their kids. At times, that's true.

But parents sometimes forget those children grow up and make their own decisions. We can't "make" them do anything.

IS MY WAY BEST?

Frank Sinatra's "My Way" is a powerful song. Whenever I hear it, i find myself singing along.

One of the key lines is: "Regrets, I've had a few. But then again, too few to mention."

Really? As I said to Joe, "We all have regrets."

I talked about how it took me several days to swing into action after my father had his stroke. I was in a state of selfish denial because I knew my life was about to get harder. As time passed, I shaped up and became the son he needed.

But at first, I dropped the ball and kicked it all over field before picking it up and running with it.

Most of us have learned doing it "My Way" is not always the

best way. We don't find that out until we walk down that wrong road for a while.

THE POWER OF FORGIVENESS

Not long after I grew more serious about my faith in the middle 1990s, I wrote letters of apology to former bosses and several people whom I'd treated unfairly. Some were absolutely stunned to receive the letters. And grateful. I made sure to point every finger of blame at myself. That led to some very good talks.

But in other cases, there was no response. That also is to be expected.

No doubt, more folks thought they should have been on that list—people whom I never realized I've hurt over the decades.

Faith's power is fueled by forgiveness. The broken heart can be healed by understanding God is willing to forgive us. From my Christian perspective, that's what the death of Jesus on the cross is about. From the Jewish background, it's Yom Kippur.

Something has to die. Blood is spilled. From that comes new life, new hope.

I told Joe, "God can forgive us even when others don't. That has always been a comfort to my heart."

Should we 'cancel' someone when we disagree?

I recently received an email from a reader informing me of "being canceled."

The reader mentioned that some writers whose opinions he didn't like wrote about things being "canceled" in society. So he was canceling them.

I was on the list because I didn't write about the topic.

Part of his email was attempted humor. But there was a bigger issue hiding behind the debate over what parts of culture are "being canceled" and who is doing the canceling.

This story isn't about that. You can find thousands of opinions online, in the paper and over the air about what should and should not be "canceled." So please don't write me about that. I don't do politics.

Instead, it's telling someone we know "you're canceled," even if we don't quite use those words.

Here's the disclaimer: There are people we know who should be "canceled," because they are abusive, dangerous, devious, etc. We are talking about bad behavior that can cause serious physical and/or emotional harm to us.

As I've written before, you can "forgive" someone, but not completely restore the destructive relationship. Forgiveness is one step, reconciliation is another. Distance from certain people can be wise.

ISN'T THAT RIGHT?

But what I'm writing about is how politics has become so toxic, it pushes us to "cancel" those in our lives whose opinions don't match ours.

Or even the fact they don't share the same passion for a cause as we do. They don't want to take up our side on this issue. That must make them a bad person, right?

And you better say . . . RIGHT.

Notice how that has slipped into our vocabulary . . . ending a sentence with RIGHT?

I'm guilty of it. I'll make statement to someone and say, "Isn't that RIGHT?"

And that person better agree with me. I didn't realize it until a friend mentioned it months ago. It's been a battle to keep that from popping out of my mouth.

Former Tribe announcer Herb Score would tell his new radio partners, "Don't say, 'Isn't that right, Herb?' What if I don't agree? We don't want to get into that on the air. It's not worth it."

Think about that phrase for a moment . . .

It's not worth it.

We argue about too much that is out of our control, too much that can "cancel" a relationship because we want to be "right."

Is it worth it?

As Proverbs 21:23 reads: "He who guards his mouth and his tongue keeps himself from calamity."

THE PUP TENT FAMILY

Too often, we are "looking to be offended." That's especially true if we're with some people who aren't exactly at the top of our mental list of favorites.

In their presence, we can seethe inside, waiting for them to say something dumb or insulting—so we can pounce on it. Or we can justify our inner loathing of them.

I know of family members who don't speak to each other

because of disagreements about elections. The issues are important. Families members have "canceled" each other over things that do not directly relate to their relationship.

We live in the age of rage, and we're told to just "say what's on your mind." Who cares if it hurts someone else? In the process, we forget all the good personal things we have been through together.

Then someone has a heart attack . . . a stroke . . . an accident.

Suddenly, those disagreements seem exactly what they are . . . petty.

When we are trying to decide if a family member needs to go into a nursing home or is facing major surgery, does it really matter who voted for what candidate or what someone thinks about a big bill in Congress?

Once upon a time, families were big tents with lots of room for different personalities and eccentricities. Now, it seems we don't even want pup tents.

LET'S GIVE IT A TRY

Over the years, I've heard from readers who have decided to "cancel" my faith columns because I don't use their quote version of the Bible.

They ignore the fact that the *Plain Dealer*/Cleveland.com is the only major daily mainstream media even willing to publish this type of faith column—and editors and management have taken some heat for it.

Jesus was consistently criticized because he didn't engage in the political debates over the Roman occupation of his homeland. He was ripped for "eating" with sinners. He spent a lot of time with people whose views didn't match his own.

When some friends start a heated political debate, I often say, "Let's not go there. Nothing we say here will change anything right now."

I remind myself, "Not every opinion on every topic has to be expressed."

We became friends because of things we had common. Our key

relationships have to be about more than the latest hot button issues. Relationships are too important to be canceled over what is fueling the latest name-calling television "news shows" with everyone screaming at once.

Or as Proverbs 12:18 reads: "Reckless words pierce like a sword, but the tongue of the wise brings healing."

A FINAL THOUGHT

After a very thoughtful and civil exchange of ideas (many from him) where we put the politics aside, I sent the reader who canceled me this note:

"Not sure what I did to you personally, but I hate to lose a reader under any circumstance. I also know that if any of us were 'canceled' when someone disagreed with us, we'd probably have no one left in our lives.

"I thank God for forgiveness from my family, my friends and my readers. At 65, it's been one of the best gifts I've received from so many."

He replied:

"I'm a 67-year-old man and I too continually ask for forgiveness. The good Lord has responded to me many times over and blessed me. I am reminded daily of Luke 23:34: 'Forgive them Father, for they know not what they do.' The verse is the epitome of asking forgiveness."

Can we really forgive and forget something so painful?

During a jail ministry service, I talked a little about forgiveness.

Afterward, a middle-aged man named Fred came up to me. He opened the shirt of his orange jump suit.

"See that scar?" he asked.

There was no way to miss it.

The scar was about 8 inches long, 4 inches across.

It was old, but you could still see how the skin was damaged and would never fully heal to look as healthy as it once did.

"What happened?" I asked.

"It was my mother," he said. "I was just a kid."

This discussion was about 10 years ago, so I don't recall all the details. But the scar came from his mother taking a hot iron to his chest.

"How do you forgive that?" he asked, his voice quiet and cracking.

He wiped a tear from his eye with his sleeve.

How *do* you forgive that?

Most of us don't have a huge physical scar near our hearts as he did, but emotional ones are there.

And they linger.

The abusive parent. The neglectful parent. The close friend or spouse who walked out, telling everyone how you are an awful person.

FORGIVE & FORGET?

And when we hear, "Just forgive and forget," who can do that? When the offense is serious, the answer is "probably no one."

Nor does the Bible say anything about forgiving and forgetting, other than God does forget our sins after they are forgiven.

That's from Hebrews 10:17-18: "Their sins and lawless acts, I will remember no more. And where these have been forgiven, there is no longer any sacrifice for sin."

Some of us have been hurt and we are waiting for the offender to "make up for it."

The "no sacrifice for sin" part does apply to us. When our lives are scarred by a major offense, we're not going to forget it. In those instances, there is really nothing that can "make up for it."

THE DEAD BODY TORTURE

Do our scars define us?

Some of us are waiting for a person to apologize or somehow "make it up to us," and that person is dead or long gone.

I've read several versions of this quote, but I like this best: "Forgiving means giving up the right to get even." How could Fred "get even" with his mother? If you have been sexually abused, how do you really "get even" with the other person?

Suddenly, we can become emotionally (and maybe even physically) jailed by our violent attempt to break free of unforgiveness.

I once heard Pastor Knute Larson (formerly of The Chapel in Akron) tell a story of long-ago torture where a person had a human corpse tied to him. He couldn't shake it free.

The disease and the insects went from the corpse to the man who was attached to it. He eventually died.

Larson said that's what long-held bitterness and resentment do to us.

WHAT TO DO?

A few key points:

Forgiveness is not forgetting.

Forgiveness doesn't mean restoring a relationship with a dangerous person.

Reconciliation is the next step after forgiving. It means redefining the relationship. Maybe it's now only casual where it was once close. Or perhaps we can talk it out.

Forgiveness is remembering the times when God has forgiven us, and others have forgiven us.

Sometimes people who have a hard time forgiving others don't believe God has forgiven them. Is that an issue?

I asked Fred, "Does the scar hurt when you touch it?"

He said it had "healed." It was still ugly, but it no longer hurt . . . at least not physically.

That's how forgiveness works when God and prayer are involved. Counseling might also be needed.

It's not a quick process. We often have to tell ourselves, "I'm not walking around carrying that dead body of bitterness on my back. It's killing me."

Eventually through the power of prayer, we can accept the scars as part of our life—but it's not going to determine how we live.

FAMILY MESS: WE ALL HAVE IT

Are you agonizing over your troubled child?

I crossed paths with an older acquaintance. We hadn't seen each other for years, and talked about jail ministry and families.

"I have two children," she said. "Twins. I mean, they were born like 10 minutes apart."

Two girls. One is now a teacher, married with kids. The other has been battling drug problems for years, in and out of jail.

She was beating herself up about the troubled daughter.

"I made some mistakes with her," she said.

Her husband left her when the children were young. She worked and raised them with the help of some extended family members.

She was in tears, worrying about her daughter whom she feared was using heroin.

"What about your other daughter?" I asked.

"She is a great kid," the woman said. "She was easy to raise. Made good decisions . . ."

"Exactly," I said, interrupting her. "She made good decisions."

She became quiet.

"Two kids," I said. "Same home. Same circumstances. Same age. If you blame yourself for your daughter and her drug use, do you give yourself credit for the daughter with a great life?"

"She was the good kid growing up," my friend said.

"Because she made good decisions," I said. "After they grow past the stage where you can physically pick them up and put them in a playpen, you really can't make your children do much of anything. They have to decide for themselves."

I then asked her to show me a picture of the "good" daughter and her family. My friend's mood changed. She glowed.

We talked about how we dwell on what went wrong and seldom really celebrate what went right.

LESSONS FROM JAIL

After more than 20 years in jail ministry, I have had a lot of conversations like this. Another man told me about his four children. One of them had been in and out of our jail ministry class. The other three all had good jobs.

You can guess what happened: He was distraught over his son with drug problems.

"Our pastor helped him get into treatment and later get a job," he said. "We have tried so hard . . ."

His voice broke, he couldn't finish the sentence.

"It's not your fault," I said. "Now look at me."

He raised his head.

"It's not your fault," I repeated. "If you had six kids and all six were in and out of jail, then we would have a different discussion. But not this time . . ."

That's what some of you reading this need to hear: IT'S NOT YOUR FAULT.

BLESSINGS & CURSES

These are two examples of many conversations over the years.

A powerful verse is Deuteronomy 30:19: "I have set before you life and death, blessings and curses. Now choose life, so that you and your children may live."

Some parents could read that verse and begin to fall into despair again. They will hear, "It's my fault" because my children are not "living right." There is another factor.

Think of the parents who have one or two children struggling, but others are doing well. The temptation is to dwell on the child with the issues and take for granted the children who made good decisions.

The "good children" long for attention and praise, even if they don't show it. They are your blessings. Like you, they have been worn down (at least to some extent) by the family member with addictions or other problems.

REMEMBER ALL YOUR KIDS

A woman once told me, "I can never feel good as long as one of my children has problems."

It's a bad idea to have your mood dictated by that child. It's also not fair to the "good kids." Why should your frustrations with the one "problem child" impact your relationship with the others?

You want to pray for all your children, and learn to pray with them. You can start any time, even if it feels uncomfortable. Pray for God's love over them. Pray for them to gain wisdom. Pray that God will show you how you can help them.

Maybe God will show you the need for an apology. If that's the case, do it immediately. It will bless the relationship. But remember, choose life as you relate to your children—especially those who are the "good kids."

Finally, give yourself a break from the blame game when it comes to those whose decisions have led to a lot of pain.

Instead of their last words, think of the life your loved one lived

"You know what was the last thing my husband said to me?"

An elderly lady was telling me this story.

What a question—the final words that someone speaks.

One of my favorites was uttered by Confederate General Stonewall Jackson: "Let us cross over the river and rest under the shade of the trees."

Jackson was a Sunday school teacher while also a professor at Virginia Military Institute before the Civil War. Perhaps he was thinking about the Jews crossing the River Jordan and entering the promised land as he took his final breath.

No matter, what Jackson said are some comforting words—as if he had a glimpse of heaven.

But that is not what my friend heard from her husband.

He said: "I'm sorry."

I waited for more, but that was it.

Two words: "I'm sorry."

She talked about how they'd had a long marriage, and how those words confused her.

I did know her husband. It did appear that they had a good marriage, as much as anyone could tell who is not in the immediate family.

But more than 10 years after the death of her husband, she was haunted by those two words.

I'm sorry . . . for what?

Was there a secret that she didn't know, something that he was ashamed about?

"I doubt it," I said.

Her husband was dying of heart failure. He had been very weak and was on medication.

The final words of Jesus on the cross ranged from "Father, forgive them for they don't know what they are doing" (Luke 23:34) to "Father, into your hands I commit my spirit."

I pray I can die with the same forgiving, trusting spirit as Jesus.

But near the end of life, it is strange what we might think about—and the regrets that might cling to us.

I talked to the lady about her husband's final day.

She said something remarkable had occurred. He had almost zero energy and had been mostly sleeping the previous few days.

But that last day, he was alert. He asked to speak to a young pastor, who had been a regular visitor during his final year. Next, he talked to his financial adviser, making sure everything was set for his wife. After that, his best friend came by.

Then he spent some time with his wife, mostly pleasant conversation.

Then came the last two words: "I'm sorry."

As I listened to the woman, I prayed for some wisdom.

One of my favorite verses is James 1:5: "If any of you lacks wisdom, you should ask God, who gives generously to all without finding fault, and it will be given to you."

I believe the holidays cause many of us to rummage through the old closets and suitcases of our lives.

And we very well may not understand everything that we take out and ponder.

"Did you ever consider that he was sorry to leave you?" I asked.

She looked at me, not understanding.

"Think about his last day," I said.

"He saw the people who meant so much to him. He put everything in place for you, and did the best he could. But he also knew that he couldn't be there for you—and that bothered him."

She smiled, considering that.

"That's something I perhaps would say to my wife," I said. "I'd be sorry to leave her."

And there was something else, something I didn't say that day.

Why look for trouble when it comes to final words? Look at the life instead, because that's the real story.

Parents, read this regardless of your kids' ages

A few years ago a man told me this story.

He was a retired professor. He had a healthy pension. His wife had died after a long illness. He had a troubled son, some of it drugs, lots of it due to blowing money.

"You won't believe this," he said. "I've got money trouble."

He lived in Michigan. His son lived in another state. Because of some decisions the professor had made when his son was young, he felt guilty about not "being there enough" for his son.

The professor said he had paid for a couple of trips to rehabilitation for his son. He also spent thousands keeping his son out of major debt.

"I've given him money," the professor said. "I've taken out loans, maxed out credit cards. I even got some of those payday loans. Right now, I can't pay my mortgage."

His family was trying to pull him away from the troubled son and help put his finances in order.

Six months after hearing that story, I heard the professor had died of a heart attack.

NOT AN UNCOMMON STORY

"The money problems of an addict in the family is something many families don't talk about," said Father Bob Stec, pastor of St. Ambrose Catholic Parish in Brunswick.

Stec has worked with families of addicts, especially those on heroin. He mentioned recently talking to six couples who were in premarital counseling.

"Two of the six had a sibling who died from heroin," said Stec. "The impact on the families is devastating. It's a terrible disease that eats away at so many people."

THE BIG LIE

The addicts not only destroy their own lives, but also cause chaos and pain to those around them.

It's why the comment, "I'm just hurting myself" by drinking or doing drugs is such a lie.

"You want to help people," said Stec. "We all do. But I have watched families go broke as they keep sending the person from one rehab center to another."

Those places can cost from $30,000 to more than $100,000.

It might not be because of drugs, but parents step into the financial mess created by their children. They co-sign for loans almost knowing they will be stuck with the payments because the child isn't dependable. But they do it anyway. They become addicted to helping, maybe out of guilt or because they enjoy being "needed" by their children.

"I've had adult children come to me and say they were now having to support their parents because the parents spent so much money on the kid in trouble," said Stec. "That creates a lot of resentment in families."

Stec talks about the spiritual battle facing families in these situations. He is involved in a movement called Greater Than Heroin at his church and elsewhere.

WHO CARES THE MOST?

Leslie Parker-Barnes is the Minister of Worship at Akron's Arlington Church of God. She also has been the leader of the Youth Excellence Performance Arts Workshop (YEPAW) with primarily inner-city youth for 32 years.

"Sometimes, love means saying, 'No,' " said Parker-Barnes.

"Love is not always soft and gooey. It's telling someone, 'I can't keep helping you hurt yourself.'"

It's tempting for parents to care about the schoolwork or the job of their kids more than the kids do themselves. In essence, parents do the work for those who need to work and learn themselves.

What they learn is that someone will bail them out.

"I've had young adults thank me for not helping them in a certain situation years ago," said Parker-Barnes. "It was hard not to do it. You want to spare them the pain."

But doing too much for the person at the wrong time just creates more pain.

YOU CAN'T MAKE ANYONE DO ANYTHING

Because we see the world a certain way, it's hard to understand why others on a destructive road fail to do the same.

"Some people are going to do what they are going to do," said Stec. "You hate to see them crash. But after you have tried to help and tried to help, you realize you can't solve the problem."

In the meantime, you can alienate others in the family. They feel forgotten.

"Kids have told me they are tired of being 'the good kid,' and taken for granted," said Parker-Barnes. "They've told me that they feel they should act up to get some attention. I've seen it happen."

Those are the children who should receive our financial support. They are the ones who may stumble in life, but have the character to get back up again.

But too often the "problem child" sucks up all the energy and resources. When the others are in need of encouragement and time, we feel empty. They lose out.

PRAYING FOR WISDOM

Parker-Barnes has told her kids: "You can always come home. Always. I don't care what you've done. You always have a home with us."

But there is a condition.

"You know the rules of the house," she said. "You have to follow them if you stay here."

Parker-Barnes insists children are looking for structure and order in their lives, even if they rebel against it at first.

None of this is easy for parents dealing with these problems.

Stec suggests parents check Relink.org. Another excellent organization is Al-Anon for families in these situations.

"The serenity prayer is important for all of us," said Stec.

I love this part of it:

"God, grant me the serenity to accept the things I cannot change. . .

The courage to change the things I can. . .

And the wisdom to know the difference. . ."

Are we playing the parent blame game?

We live in the age of blaming our parents—or another authority figure.

In a Psychology Today article, Eileen Kennedy-Moore wrote: "In therapy offices and casual conversations, it's common to hear people complain about how their parents 'messed them up.' Maybe the parents were too hovering or uninvolved, too strict or too permissive, too critical or too unaware, too demanding or not demanding enough. Or maybe the parents just weren't 'there' for them in a way the adult child wished."

That's so true. Every parent knows the feeling: "Am I trying to do too much for the kids, or is it not enough?" There are many adults who still blame their parents for their problems.

Here's the disclaimer: This column is not about those of us who had self-destructive addicts for parents or suffered physical and/or sexual abuse. Some of us had parents with severe mental problems. One of my friends barely knew her mother because she was in and out of psychiatric facilities.

Another friend lost her father at a young age. Her mother continually had different men living in the house, some tried to abuse her.

So as you read this, keep in mind it's not about these types of extreme cases. Counseling, prayer and perhaps medical treatment might be needed in these situations.

But the general "parent blame game" is played too often by too many.

"I hear it all the time," said the Rev. Bob Stec, pastor of St. Ambrose Catholic Parish in Brunswick.

Stec mentioned a woman who blamed her alcoholic father for her marrying a woman who also was an alcoholic. The discussion took many turns. One was about how her husband wanted both of them to stop drinking.

"But she didn't want to give up having her glass of wine," said Stec. "The drinking was his problem, she said. There was a lot of unforgiveness, and that's often at the heart of blaming the parents."

WHOSE FAULT IS IT?

"Adult children sometimes blame their parents for everything negative in their lives: lack of motivation, poor self-confidence, work uncertainty, overwork, fears, anger, feeling lonely, relationship break-ups, and more," wrote Kennedy-Moore.

Of course, parents impact our lives.

"But there are times in everyone's life when we must say, 'I choose to be different than my parents,'" said Stec. "Otherwise, we are stuck in the past."

My parents often had heated and long arguments, followed by even longer and more strained periods of frozen silence. Before we were married, my wife, Roberta, and I talked about it. She saw some of it in my parents. We were determined not to carry that into our marriage—and we didn't.

We can disagree, even argue a bit, but not scream, call names and continually dig up past offenses. I watched all of that destructive behavior while growing up.

Consider the woman who was raised with alcoholism, then married a man who liked to drink and then blamed her father. Some would argue, "Well, that's all she knew."

But wasn't her heart telling her that something was terribly wrong with all the drinking?

"We have the power to choose to be different," repeated Stec. "And that power comes through Christ. It takes prayer. It takes forgiveness of our parents, too."

We live in a society that prefers to judge people in their worst moments.

"Are we looking to be offended?" asked Stec. "It comes down to forgiveness. So often, we forget how often God has forgiven us. Or how often others have shown us mercy and grace. We should keep track of that, not just our own hurts."

Parents can have several children. Some turn out well, others are angry and troubled. You hear them discuss the same parents— and the stories are completely different. You can't believe they came from the same family.

Stec talked a lot about forgiveness, and that can be hard in families. Jealousy often is a factor. We can believe parents favored a sibling over us. Sometimes, that does happen. But how about this thought, especially for those of us who are parents: "How do you want your kids to judge you?"

OK, now view your own parents through that same big-picture lens and see if some of your own problems from decades ago now appear a little smaller.

Our parents are like us—people with strengths, people with problems and people who need forgiveness.

When a crisis brings healing

I was talking to a friend about her mother, who just turned 80.

Nine years ago, her mother went through a stroke and later major heart surgery.

"We are closer now than ever," she said.

We talked about her mother's birthday party at a nursing home. She visits her mother five days a week. They talk on the phone daily. For several years after the stroke, her mother lived in her home until more care was needed.

"I love her so much," my friend said.

"Do you think you'd be close if she hadn't had the stroke?" I asked.

"No," she said. "It's been so hard. But it has dramatically changed our relationship."

Her mother has said the same thing. The stroke was a life-changer for both of them. It's a draining physical hardship for the mother and a major emotional burden for both of them.

But had it never happened, their relationship would lack the depth it has today. The old emotional wounds and resentments would still be bleeding.

Through a crisis, a healing has come.

Thankful for the stroke? On the surface, of course not.

But without it, their relationship would still be a source of pain rather than the comfort of today.

My friend knows someone who has had to step up and help with her parents in a long-term care situation.

"It's the hardest thing you'll ever do," my friend told her friend. "But you'll never regret it."

I feel the same way.

A PERSONAL STORY

Why write about this during Thanksgiving weekend?

Earlier in the week, I wrote a column thanking the readers.

I opened with my friend's story because it's much like my own story—and the stories of others in my age range.

In 1993, my father had a major stroke. I was so naive about it, I had no idea that strokes hitting the left side of the brain can impair a person's speech. That happened to my father. His vocabulary was reduced to a single word—"man." Sometimes, it was "Oh, man!"

The left side of the brain also controls the right side of the body. My father lost the use of his right hand and leg—and he was right-handed. Brushing teeth, eating—almost anything requiring his right hand became an ordeal.

There were times when tears came down from feeling helpless.

My friend's mother didn't lose her speech. Her left side is paralyzed. She draws with her right hand and has discovered she has artistic talent. She is thankful for that.

My father was great with numbers. But that disappeared with the stroke. So did his ability to read. It was a long, nearly five-year ordeal with my father before he died on his 78th birthday.

Anyone in a major long-term care situation knows about helping someone get dressed and even go to the bathroom. They discovered the need to cut up food, dealing with doctors and pharmacies.

There are those late nights staring at the ceiling wondering, "How can I can face another day?"

Would I want my father to go through that again? No.

Am I thankful it happened? Yes.

LESSON FROM THE STROKE

As you read this section, it can apply to any crisis—not just strokes. I have friends whose lives have changed for the better in an emotional and spiritual sense while dealing with cancer, dementia, a major disabling injury and a special-needs child.

Before my father's stroke, I believed in God mostly as the Grand Designer. I went to church for moral guidance, and sort of like brushing my teeth. It's good for me—but no real emotional attachment.

During those stroke years, I had to face the question, "Is God real or not?" It was when I discovered it didn't matter how many books I'd written or awards I'd won—the big question was, "What can I do to help my father find some peace?"

There were nights when I was angry at God, asking, "Why did my father have to go through this?" But the real question was, "Why did I have to go through this? It's messing up my life!"

I felt like this from the start of Psalm 13:

"How long, O Lord? Will you forget me forever? How long will you hide your face from me?

"How long must I take counsel in my soul and have sorrow in my heart all the day?"

THE DARK NIGHT OF THE SOUL

Most people in this situation go through what St. John of the Cross called, "The Dark Night of the Soul." It's when a sense of despair and doom seem to be closing in.

What happens next is what matters.

Through frustrations and sorrow, I grew closer to God. I had a friend challenge me to read the Bible. He guided me through different parts. My wife already was close to God, but the stroke did bring us closer together as a couple.

Growing closer also means being hit with a new set of stress and conflicts that comes with a crisis—and learning how to deal with it and each other.

l often leaned on Psalm 34:18:

"The Lord is close to the brokenhearted and saves those who are crushed in spirit."

Going through my father's stroke brought me closer to God and him. It also was a way for him to see how much I loved and appreciated him.

A few days before he died, we talked about some family history. I knew he was bitter about some things that had happened. I asked if he wanted to pray for God to give him forgiveness, help him forgive some others and find some peace.

He nodded, tears in his eyes.

We prayed. He lived five more days, and it seemed light had broken through some of the darkness of his soul and he finally found the peace that only God can give.

THE CIVIL WAR
AND US

In a roadside grave, a mystery about a Confederate soldier

BROWNS GAP, VA.—One gravestone.

That's what I found along Browns Gap Road.

It's really not much of a road, at least as we know it. It's grass and dirt as it cuts through the Shenandoah Mountains in the southern section of the national park.

My wife, Roberta, and I hiked part of this road . . . the same road first built in 1805.

And it's the same road where Stonewall Jackson drove his Confederate troops from one end of the Shenandoah Mountains to the other on May 2, 1862.

He did it again from June 9-12, 1862, allowing them to camp along the way. Browns Gap is a footnote in Civil War history. Jackson used it to mount sneak attacks miles away in the Shenandoah Valley.

As we walked along the road on a sunny November afternoon, there was a small dirt path heading up a rocky hill. I knew what I would find—the grave.

Hiking guides mention that the grave of William Howard is right off the road.

Other men are buried along this road, but only one grave is marked.

It's WILLIAM W. HOWARD, CSA . . . COMPANY F, 44TH INFANTRY.

THE MAN

Little is known about Howard.

Military records show that on June 12, 1861, a William Howard joined the Confederate Infantry in Fluvanna County—not far from Charlottesville, home of the University of Virginia.

Not only did Howard join, but so did his two brothers—Napoleon and John.

According to a blog called Rightside Va, John Howard died on Aug. 1, 1861. He was 19. Cause of death is listed as "typhoid." He died in Monterey, Virginia, and that's where he is buried.

It's about 50 miles from where William is buried.

William died on Oct. 1, 1861 . . . also of typhoid. He was 21.

William supposedly died at Camp Allegheny, in what was then Virginia and now is West Virginia—at least 60 miles away.

And this was in 1861.

From the little research I did, there is no indication of Confederate troops using Browns Gap until Jackson's men did so in May 1862.

Did they hang on to a dead body for eight months? Hard to believe.

In fact, I'm not sure how much of this information is accurate because records are understandably iffy from so long ago.

THE MYSTERY

Maybe Howard isn't buried there. Maybe his lone surviving brother (Napoleon) decided to put up a tombstone as he camped along Browns Gap road.

But I've seen lots of Confederate tombstones, and Howard's is exactly like many of those you find in larger battlefields.

I found myself thinking, "Only God knows what really happened here."

That's so true about so much in life . . . and death . . . even about people whom we think we know well.

There are parts of their lives that are mysteries, things they did that can't be explained.

And dreams that were destroyed.

When the three Howard brothers joined up with a group called the Fluvanna Hornets in the summer of 1861, did any of them imagine that two of them would be dead only a few months later—of typhoid?

Or that the one surviving brother—Napoleon—wouldn't fall to typhoid. He lived long enough to fight at Gettysburg, where he was captured by Union soldiers. He was imprisoned in Maryland and released after the war.

When you hike with the Shenandoah Mountains looming so large, you feel very small.

This is God's country, where you find a lonely tombstone of a 19-year-old who died more than 150 years ago.

Some of us still have our loved ones with us—people we can talk with who can tell us about who we are and where we came from. Don't hesitate to talk to them while you still have the chance.

Crossing Antietam Creek:
Bridges to devastation as well as to recovery and forgiveness

SHARPSBURG, MD.—The bridge was right in front of me.

I stood where a young man named Henry Kingsbury did on September 17, 1862. He was a colonel in the Union Army. His job was to lead his troops over what is now known as the Burnside Bridge at Antietam National Battlefield.

Back then, it was just a bridge over what was called Antietam Creek. That's a big misnomer. This is a respectable river in this part of Western Maryland.

Kingsbury knew there were a lot of Confederate soldiers on the other side of the bridge, hiding on several hillsides. He had no idea how many men were there.

If you stand on the bridge when it's eerily silent, as it was when I was there, you can hear the whisper of the creek flowing down. You look across the bridge and realize, it's a little like life.

You know you are supposed to cross it.

You think it looks rather peaceful, but there are major problems ahead.

You have seen others try to cross and falter.

If you stare hard at the different bridges you face at different stages in your life, you have to admit it's a bit scary.

It could be taking care of a child or being responsible for someone who is ill. It could be any bridge that suddenly confronts us and we know it's our duty to try to cross it.

What Kingsbury didn't know is that the little hill he saw on the other side of the bridge with a few men shooting at him was a tease. He had no idea that one of the Confederate officers on the opposite hillside was David Jones. They were close friends. Kingsbury had married the sister-in-law of Jones.

Now they were at war against each other, having no idea they were on the opposite sides of this bridge.

Welcome to the Civil War, which ripped apart friends and families.

Kingsbury went with the North, partly because Union General Ambrose Burnside was his legal guardian after the death of Kingsbury's father in 1856. Yes, the same Burnside who was in charge of taking the bridge and attacking the flank of the Confederate Army.

YOU CAN'T MAKE UP LIFE

Burnside was never able to lead his men across the bridge.

They were put in a terrible position by their generals, and were mowed down by a barrage of bullets.

Kingsbury was shot four times. He was taken to a house serving as a crude field hospital.

Burnside heard about Kingsbury's condition and rushed to the house. After he arrived, Burnside learned Kingsbury had told the surgeons to deal with other men. The young man knew his wounds were fatal.

Burnside talked to Kingsbury quite a while before he died.

Kingsbury was 26.

Meanwhile, on the hillside was Jones, a native of South Carolina, who went with the Confederates.

He later heard his men had killed his friend and distant relative.

Ethan S. Rafuse wrote *A Battlefield Guide to Antietam, South Mountain and Harpers Ferry*.

"When he learned of Kingsbury's death, Jones was grief-stricken," wrote Rafuse. "There is speculation this event contributed to his fatal stroke, only a few months after Antietam."

The man who ordered the attack (Burnside) caused the death

of his stepson (Kingsbury). The man who ordered his men to fire on Kingsbury's troops was his close friend (Jones). And not long afterward, depressed, Jones died.

Many of us have family stories like that, of decisions seemingly made for the right reasons that lead to terrible consequences.

THE POWER OF FORGIVENESS

My wife, Roberta, and I walked a few of the trails of this battle-field.

We have been here several times over the years. We like walking the trails. Most lead away from the tourist areas into the heart of the woods, the fields and the quiet.

We climbed a hill where a few old cannons were posted.

Down the way, there was a field with a few deer in a place where there were more than 22,000 casualties on a single day. It's considered the bloodiest 24 hours in American history.

While today we don't have actual battlefields, we do have family messes.

But we also can recover. Often it takes the power of prayer. It's takes going to God for forgiveness. It may require more than a few tears and some people to help you.

At Antietam, cannons are silent. The creek is peaceful. The dead on both sides are equally remembered with dignity. And forgiveness is more important than ever.

The Fourth of July, a search for shoes and the Civil War

It started with a search for shoes.

That's how former *Plain Dealer* and *Cleveland Press* columnist Don Robertson sized up the Battle of Gettysburg in his 1959 novel, "The Three Days." Good luck finding a copy.

While far more people know of Michael Shaara's 1975 Pulitzer Prize winner *The Killer Angels* when it comes to novels about Gettysburg, it was Robertson's work that I read in the early 1970s that brought the Civil War alive to me.

You probably heard of the Battle of Gettysburg. You may know it lasted from July 1-3, 1863—although General Robert E. Lee didn't fully withdraw his Confederate troops until July 4. In the three days, "as many as 51,000 soldiers from both armies were killed, wounded, captured or missing," according to the American Battlefield Trust.

It's a battle where more than 165,000 soldiers from the North and South poured into little Gettysburg, Pennsylvania, a town of 2,400. It's where the townspeople hid in their barns and basements. It's where free African Americans went into the woods— terrified they'd be captured by the Confederates and taken to the South as slaves.

It's when Abraham Lincoln sat in the White House, awaiting telegrams and other information from the battle—knowing the Republic could be lost if the Union failed to stop Lee as the Fourth of July loomed.

SHOES OR NO SHOES MISSES THE POINT

Civil War scholars love to debate the "search for shoes" theme as the reason for the battle because Gettysburg had no shoe factory. Ten significant roads went through or close to the town, and that's the reason for the battle, some claim.

But Confederate General Henry Heth was searching for shoes for his troops, and wrote as much after the war. Let's have some compassion for the confused general. He graduated last in his 1847 class at West Point.

"He fought in the Battle of Chancellorsville, though without major distinction," according to the American Battlefield Trust. He also wasn't supposed to engage with the Union Army if he ran into them during his scouting mission near Gettysburg, but he did so anyway.

Lee thought the battle would happen near the much larger town of Harrisburg. Union General George Meade believed the battle would happen elsewhere, not Gettysburg.

SO MANY WHAT IFS

Had the Union not promoted Meade, they probably would have lost this battle with their inept previous generals. Had Lee listened to fellow Gen. James Longstreet and not ordered Pickett's Charge, where 6,000 of his troops were killed or wounded in less than an hour. . .

Had a Bowdoin College professor turned Union officer named Joshua Chamberlain not seized the high ground at Little Round Top to stop the Confederates on July 2 . . .

We could be looking at a much different country today.

REMEMBERING OUR HISTORY

Now, we watch fireworks. We have cookouts. We visit friends, perhaps watch ballgames. The Fourth of July is a holiday that seemingly has little meaning for too many of us.

But this accidental battle helped save the Union. In fact, the

Civil War should have soon come to an end not long after July 4, 1863. Because as Lee was taking what was left of his ravaged army back to Virginia, the Union had found its general. His name was U.S. Grant.

On that same July 4, 1863, Grant captured Vicksburg, Mississippi. That gave the Union control of the Mississippi River and convinced Lincoln to put Grant in charge of the entire Union Army.

Now too many people judge these men from the 1860s by the standards of the 2000s. There is no historical context, little realization of the price paid to end slavery and save the Union—620,000 died, which would be like 6 million today if you consider the percentage of the country's population.

Yes, Jim Crow and other discriminatory laws came later. Lincoln would not live long enough to celebrate July 4, 1865. He was assassinated and died on April 15, 1865. The country could have collapsed then.

But it didn't—which is something to remember.

Ours remains an imperfect Union. But it's still a Union, and there's much to be said for that.

SPECIAL
PLACES

Sunsets, God and Lake Erie

Even when I was going to church with the same enthusiasm that I used to brush my teeth, I knew there was a God . . . somewhere.

And I felt God's powerful presence when watching the sun set over places such as Lake Erie. I asked my readers on Facebook about it.

That led to Tanya Baldwin Foose writing, "God lives at the line where the water and the sky meet."

Just like I believe God's signature can be seen in every sunset. Every night, they are different.

In Northern Ohio, we are blessed because we live reasonably close to one of the truly great lakes.

You can argue that Lake Superior (my favorite great lake) or spots on the ocean have even more dramatic views, but the big point is this from Michael Roberts: "I love Lake Erie so much. It may sound corny, but I truly feel at one with the universe when I'm on a seashore (salt or otherwise)."

Recently, my wife, Roberta, and I have gone up to the lake to walk the beach and swim a bit. We went to Huron (Nickle Plate Beach) and Ashtabula Harbor (Walnut Beach). One east, one west of Cleveland. Both about an hour away from our home in Akron.

We had not done this for years and realized what we've been missing.

AS THE SUN GOES DOWN . . .

This came from Mark Zimmerman:

"One evening in 2016, I was at the lowest point in my life. And then, this sunset happened at Lake Erie Bluffs in Perry. I felt as small as I've ever felt, and was reminded again of the God who is in control the greatness of what I was seeing ('the clouds rolled back as a scroll'), and cared for the smallest details of my life. A month later, I was climbing out of the valley. And thankful."

Zimmerman was using a line from Revelation 6:14: "The heavens receded like a scroll being rolled up, and every mountain and island was removed from its place."

There is the power of light turning to dark and then light again. Sometimes, the sun lights up the sky brighter than at any point in the day right before it sets. Darkness drops, and it's as if "every mountain and island" disappears.

John Basch wrote about sitting in a Bay Village picnic area near Cahoon Creek listening to the song "I Can Only Imagine" by Mercy Me. Among the lyrics are these words: "I can only imagine what it will be like when I walk by Your side . . . I can only imagine what my eyes would see . . . When Your face is before me . . . I can only imagine."

The sunsets can be a glimpse of heaven. But there also is the sunrise.

"I go early in the morning to Breakwater Beach in Geneva," wrote Carol Janes. "I love to be alone there listening to the surf and watching the sky, clouds and birds. .. It's where I pray."

Patty White also likes Geneva and wrote, "On a clear day, you can see downtown Cleveland."

THE POWER AND THE GLORY

Mankind can control a lot of things, but not "the rising of the sun or the going down of the same," as it says in Psalm 113:3.

The lake, the sunrises and sunsets, and yes, the storms remind us of God's power.

You can watch a million sunsets and sunrises and they are like people in this regard—every one is slightly different.

"The heavens declare the glory of God; the skies proclaim the work of his hands," as it says in Psalm 19:1.

Michael Mills wrote he often goes to Port Clinton and walks the beach while listening to the Rosary.

Charles Tillie wrote he went to Edgewater Park to watch the sunset on the one-year anniversary of his father's death. It's where his father took a sunset photo not long after Tillie's grandfather died, telling his son, "That's dad riding off."

HEAD TO THE LAKE!

Maybe this makes you want to head to Lake Erie. Many readers suggested their favorite Lake Erie spots. I can't list them all, but here are some:

Camp Luther, just west of Conneaut—Rick Jensen.

Lots of votes for Mentor Headlands—Jay Schmidt, Richard Ferrell, Dana Perusek and others.

Lakeside near Marblehead—Tim Schlotter, Carol Gardian Apple.

The mile-long Lorain Pier—Gregory Hardwick.

Beulah Beach between Huron and Vermilion on Route 6.—Thomas Moyers.

Finding answers in Michigan's Upper Peninsula

CHAMPION, MICH.—I've seen the signs for years: MOOSE CROSS-ING, NEXT 35 MILES.

There are supposed to be moose in Michigan's Upper Peninsula. At least 500, perhaps a thousand.

Maybe you've heard of the town of Newberry, Michigan. Then again, probably not. Newberry is the "Official Moose capital of Michigan." The 2002 Michigan statehouse and senate agreed to make Newberry the state's moose capital.

If only we could see a tremendous show of non-partisan politics like that today.

Newberry was hoping for a tourist bump with its new moose fame. The town does have a major prison. It is on the way to beautiful Tahquamenon Falls State Park.

But moose?

I have my doubts. Having come to the Upper Peninsula every summer for about 20 years, I've stopped in Newberry and asked people if they've seen a moose. You get responses like these:

"I haven't, but my cousin saw one a few years ago."

"I haven't, but I heard from a guy who talked to a guy who saw a mother and a baby moose."

"I know they're here, I just haven't seen one."

You get the idea. A little research also reveals Newberry probably is not a prime moose sighting location.

"Another Michigan city claims to be the moose capital,

although the DNR (Department of Natural Resources) has determined there are only 100 moose in the Eastern U.P.," wrote Bill Ziegler in the latest issue of Woods-N-Water News.

But Newberry is a nice little town to visit with a cool moose-themed store called the U.P. Trading Company along with Timber Charlie's, a classic U.P. restaurant with whitefish and lots of meat dishes.

WHERE THE MOOSE ARE LOOSE?

The best place to see moose in the Upper Peninsula?

It's in the area of Van Riper State Park near Champion, about 30 miles from Marquette. The literature proclaims: "A slow drive through the north of the park may reward you with the sight of a majestic moose!"

Well . . . maybe.

This is the area of the great Moose Lift. In 1985, there were 59 moose from Ontario transported to the Van Riper park area via helicopters and trucks to establish a herd. Moose had vanished from the U.P. over the years.

My wife, Roberta, and I have driven through the area. Hiked several trails. Granted, moose tend to be more active early in the morning and late at night and those are not our best hiking times.

We've seen wild turkeys. We've spotted sandhill cranes. We even ran across a peacock.

But I am starting to think moose just don't like us.

MOOSE ARE STRANGE

According to a folder called MOOSE INFORMATION handed out in the Moose Capital of Newberry, a moose "doesn't sweat," but can swim "6 mph without a break for two hours and run up to 35 mph."

A moose has longer front legs than back legs. A moose spends most of its time "eating," according to Animal Diversity Web.

These creatures stand more than 6 feet and weigh more than 1,000 pounds. So how come you can't find them?

"I post many photos of moose taken in the Upper Peninsula on Facebook and Michigan nature group sites," wrote Ziegler, the outdoor writer. "And every time I do, I hear from one or more frustrated nature enthusiasts who has tried to see a Michigan moose and failed."

But Ziegler made another point—there is so much to see in the Upper Peninsula, it should be about more than moose. Just keep your eyes open.

A LEARNING JOURNEY

What does this have to do with faith?

If you like animal metaphors, the search for the elusive moose can be like something we have prayed for . . . and worked for.

Many of us have prayed for someone with a long-term illness to be healed, but the healing never came.

John Zaccardelli recently emailed this after reading my column on the "Dark Night of the Soul."

"In my situation, there really was a miracle. The miracle wasn't my wife being healed of Alzheimer's. Rather, the miracle was that after she died, I began doing Alzheimer's Support Groups. I led Grief Share classes at my church. I began doing a Bible study at my home and at my church. I was the recipient of the miracle— taking me from a place of complacency to a place of trusting in God."

Having been through a major stroke with my father and a long-term nursing home care with my "mom" Melva, I was given real-life classes in dealing with those struggles.

One of the benefits of our moose search is the closeness my wife and I have developed. Our time together in the wilderness has made us stronger—and better equipped to handle what God brings our way.

Far from home but closer to God

I don't think much about heaven, other than that I want to go there.

There are some images of heaven with angels floating on clouds and playing harps, or perhaps of heaven as a never-ending church service where people sing and pray until they drop.

I don't know what heaven will be like, but I doubt either of those portraits is correct.

Last Saturday, I flew to Denver to cover the Browns game. I'm not sure what that 27-6 loss to Denver was; it sure wasn't heaven.

But the day before that game, I went to southern Wyoming and thought a lot about heaven.

I drove down roads where I saw more pronghorn antelope than I did cars and people. I drove down roads where I saw signs reading, "Next services, 34 miles." I drove down roads where, when it snows, they drop gates and close the interstates until the storm passes.

I drove down roads under high skies and huge clouds that seemed to rise up to the heavens. I drove down roads through miles of open pastures, roads where my cellphone was long out of range.

I drove down roads that made me think of a line from novelist Dan O'Brien: "You have a sense that everyone can see you, but no one is looking."

That may bother some people, who are uneasy about all the rugged, lonely hills and valleys.

For those who love a crowd and the 50-percent-off sale at the mall, a state with 522,830 people and an estimated 550,000 antelope might not have much appeal. I have been to Wyoming at least a dozen times. On each visit, I think how the land is not tamed by man. Some mountains are too high, some rivers too wild, some storms too fierce.

I know that there are days when Wyoming can seem like hell on earth during a blizzard, a dust storm, or with a blown radiator in the middle of nowhere and no one around to call for help.

But I didn't think of that as I drove south of Laramie.

I saw several herds of pronghorns—10 over here, 25 there, at least 50 ahead on top of the hill.

For 10 miles, not a single car was on the road.

In Isaiah 65:17, God says, "Behold, I will create a new heaven and a new earth."

I had a taste of it as I drove west on Wyoming 130 into the Snowy Mountains. They rose 10,000 feet with the sun peeking behind snow-capped peaks.

Rather than spend any time wondering how such a place was created, I was in awe of God's hand and power behind it all.

Then I saw a truck on the other side of the road, a man standing near it, staring into the woods.

I slowed down and spotted a huge horse with antlers . . . only, it was a moose in a clearing.

I stopped and walked over to the man.

"There's four of 'em," he said.

Then a female moose and two young ones ambled out from behind some bushes, joining the big bull. We watched them silently for about five minutes, me wondering what exactly got into God when he created a strange creature like a moose. Sheer entertainment, I suppose.

Finally, the four moose disappeared back in the woods.

The other man and I left, too, nodding to each other but not saying a word.

First Corinthians 2:9 reads: "As it is written: 'No eye has seen, no ear has heard, no mind has conceived what God has prepared for those who love him.' "

But that Saturday in Wyoming, I was given just a glimpse.

A scouting trip to the hills, a rushed wedding, a life lesson

It's been at least 50 years since I thought of this story, so it's hard to trust my memory.

But it came back to me on Feb. 7. That was both the date of my father's birth and his death—78 years later.

Had he lived, Tom Pluto would now be 102.

Maybe this happens to you. Maybe on the anniversary or death of someone close to you, there comes a memory. It's like finding an old cigar box in the attic. As you open the lid, you slice through a few spider webs. Then there's something inside, someone that you had forgotten long ago.

It was the middle 1960s. Along with working at old Fisher Foods, my father was a "bird dog" scout for the Cleveland Indians. There was no pay. He received a pass to all Tribe home games for two. Admission price was 50 cents each, general admission.

But my father did go to amateur games. He found some players. He didn't have the power to sign anyone. He could pass along their names to Paul O'Dea, who was in charge of the Tribe's scouting department. My father pushed the Tribe to sign Parma product and Kent State star Rich Rollins.

The Tribe skipped Rollins. Minnesota didn't. Rollins had a 10-year big-league career. He made two All-Star teams. We'd talk to Rollins after games when he came to town with the Twins.

"The Indians didn't like Rollins because he was stocky and wore glasses," my father said more than once. "They didn't think he looked like a ballplayer, but he sure played like one."

THE SCOUTING TRIP

One day, my father said, "We're going to Pennsylvania."

We drove down some two-lane blacktop roads snaking through coal country. I remember some polka music on the radio. My father was a first-generation Slovak and loved polkas.

Along the way, my father told me about a friend from the Army. His name is lost in my memory, other than a nickname, something like "Triddy."

During World War II, they played on a couple of service teams that had a lot of former and current pros.

Two big-leaguers were Willard Marshall and Johnny Beazley. Marshall made three All-Star teams after the war. Beazley had a 21-6 record with a 2.13 ERA in 1942 before entering the service. When he came home, he had a bad arm and was never the same pitcher.

"Triddy was a good as Beazley," my father said. "I saw him strike out Willard Marshall. Triddy played some pro ball, but he'd get homesick and leave his minor-league team."

My father had told me that story a few times, always ending with a shake of the head. My father played one year of independent minor-league ball in West Virginia before the war. He knew he wasn't good enough for the majors.

"But Triddy, he could have made it," said my father, shaking his head. "He had a great forkball."

The trip was about more than seeing an old Army buddy.

"Triddy's son is a very good high school pitcher," my dad said. "We're going to talk to him."

NEVER SAW THIS COMING

When we arrived at the small town in the Western Pennsylvania hills, it was almost dark. I remember going to a very small house. It had to be tiny because we lived in a very modest home in Parma—which looked like a mansion compared to Triddy's place.

My father and Triddy were thrilled to see each other. We sat in a cramped kitchen at a small aluminum table. I recall the odor of stuffed cabbage lingering.

"Tom, we're having a wedding," Triddy said. "The boy is getting married."

My father said he could still play pro ball, assuming he could talk the Indians into signing him.

"Tom, he's going to have to support a family," Triddy said. "We got him a union job at the mill." The mill where Triddy worked.

THE REARVIEW MIRROR OF LIFE

I remember asking my dad why Triddy's son couldn't play pro ball.

"He just can't," my father said. "That's how it is." He said nothing else.

Now, I realize the son's girlfriend was pregnant. The wedding was rushed.

I recall my father being quiet on the ride home. I never remember him saying much about Triddy after that. I have no idea what happened to his son.

Why this story came back to me after so many years is strange.

I know this is a strange faith column, but there is some faith at work in this. You do your duty. You take care of your family. You may grumble and complain, but you get up each day and go to work. On Sunday, you go to church.

A place that God created to remind us who's in control

AU TRAIN, MICH.—I could easily write about how watching an orange, fiery ball of a sunset over Lake Superior attests to the power of God. That is true. It also is very warm and fuzzy, and worthy of a picture postcard.

But spending nearly two weeks in Michigan's Upper Peninsula speaks to me of God's power in a much different way.

My wife, Roberta, and I have made at least six trips to the U.P. in the last seven years. We love this place. The shoreline is spectacular, the hiking challenging, the wilderness aptly named.

The first time we came here was in late June. That's when we encountered the bugs.

They really aren't bugs, they are like Blackhawk helicopters that swirl around your head. Those are just the mosquitoes. Then come the stable flies and the black flies. They travel in packs of millions and can suck the blood out of a bear in about 15 seconds. Then there are ticks.

OK, most of the bugs are not that bad. Only a few will actually kill you. The rest just make you wish you were dead.

By August, the worst of them are gone, but the bears still prowl.

Most years, there is a story that begins with someone who just pulled a blueberry pie out of the oven. It's always blueberry because they love blueberries here. They have blueberry festivals.

Bears also worship blueberries. So, as the story goes, the bear smells the blueberry pie, smashes the kitchen window and eats its prize.

Unless you happen to have a bazooka around the house, not much can stop a bear from coming through the window after a pie. But not even a bazooka can stall the big black flies or the little sneaky "no-see-ums." Although you can't see them, you can hear them buzz until you want to stick your head in a bear's mouth and just end it.

The good thing is the snow eventually comes and wipes out the bugs. It also causes the bears to sleep for months.

The bad thing is that the snow comes.

The eastern part of the U.P. receives about 200 inches per year. That's a mere dusting, say those in the western part. They insist 300 inches of snow is a good winter. They put little flags on top of their mailboxes and car antennas so they can be spotted when buried in a snow drift that seems taller than the Terminal Tower.

What Yoopers (that's what they call themselves) have learned is that so much of life can't be controlled. During one of their 2-feet-in-12-hours blizzards—with whiteouts—people just don't drive. They barely step outside. They just wait until it's over.

I don't like to wait for anything—but especially not for the weather to change.

Many Yoopers live near Lake Superior, which is about the size of South Carolina. Its average depth is 482 feet. Its average temperature is about 40 degrees. It has caused more than 350 shipwrecks. People drown every year in its vicious riptides.

It also is the world's largest freshwater lake by surface area. And it's so clear that you can watch the muskies swim up and bite your toes off. (I've never seen that happen, I've just heard stories about it.)

This summer, a moose wandered into a park in downtown Marquette and refused to leave for more than week. They just don't listen, those moose.

The Yoopers love to tell these stories about bears and bugs and moose and foot-eating fish just to watch the faces of the "trolls."

We are the trolls—anyone who lives below the Mackinac Bridge.

This is a land of 16,412 square miles and fewer than 300,000 people. The county where I'm staying—Alger—has a population of 9,601 spread over 912 square miles.

The U.P. is a place of rugged beauty, wild weather and gritty people.

It's also a place where God reminds us who is in charge—and it's surely not us.

SPECIAL
PEOPLE

John Adams' funeral and looking for the 'Power of Today'

The power of simple gestures—reaching out to let others know you care, volunteering, patience, being faithful . . . each day is a blessing, each day is a chance.

I'm writing this on Feb. 7.

That was the date my father was born—in 1920.

It also was the date he died—in 1998.

And a week ago, I was a pallbearer for the funeral of John Adams, the legendary drummer for 49 years at Tribe games.

The older you are, it's likely you spend more times at wakes, and perhaps carry caskets. At a certain age, you can become consumed by losses—deaths, broken relationships, career frustrations and health troubles.

It's like staring at the wreckage of life in the rearview mirror of life. At 71 years old, Adams had spent his last two years in a nursing home dealing with a tidal wave of health problems.

"John's middle name was Joseph," said his friend, Vicky Atrida, at the funeral Mass. "It should be changed to Volunteer."

A FAN IS A VOLUNTEER

Adams banged the drum for nearly 3,900 Tribe games over 49 years. He worked at AT&T for 41 years. He also taught disabled students to swim at Cleveland State for 40 years, and did it for free. He volunteered for various charities and musical groups. He never was paid to bang a drum for the Tribe. He did receive free tickets, but always considered himself "a fan."

What is a fan? It's someone who volunteers to follow a certain team.

In the end, he "volunteered" to be friendly and patient with the aides at the nursing home. He'd tell you that it wasn't always a successful endeavor.

But I saw him with those people. He volunteered to be a decent guy each day.

I thought about that as his funeral Mass was spiced up with drum beats and bagpipes. You could feel Adams' heartbeat.

NOT PERFECT, BUT FAITHFUL

There's a gospel song called "It's Working" by William Murphy. One of the lines is: "I haven't been perfect, but I sure been faithful . . ."

"God's got a purpose . . . yes . . . and I know He's able . . . "

As we get older, we realize the truth of Psalm 144:4: "They (people's lives) are like a breath, their days are like a fleeting shadow."

In a few weeks, it will be spring training in Arizona. Doesn't it seem like the baseball season just ended?

This is not meant to be depressing, but to face reality. Yes, "a person's days are determined," as it says in Job 14:5.

I'm not going to debate how those "days are determined," but "no one gets out of life alive," as Paul Newman said in the 1963 movie *Hud*.

Regardless of our age, the question is beyond, "What will we do with the rest of our days?" We have to keep in mind that God has a purpose, as the song goes, especially when we are faithful.

Not perfect . . . faithful.

I thought about that when talking to Paul Hoynes after the Adams funeral. Hoynes is cleveland.com's veteran baseball writer. We mentioned losing media friends Joe Tait, Les Levine and Matt Loede in the past few years.

My guess is many of you readers have your own lists of friends/ relatives who have recently died.

WILL WE BE A VOLUNTEER?

Adams was a superstar volunteer right up to the end of his life. It's not about big things. It's about doing something.

Most of us can "volunteer" to at least call or text someone who needs to hear an encouraging word. We can "volunteer" to visit someone, perhaps in a long-term care facility. If you're in a place like that, you can "volunteer" to cheer up someone who is hurting—even if you are in pain.

I speak from experience as I'm visiting a nursing home least four days a week. Usually, no longer than for 30 to 45 minutes, but I show up.

Not perfect, but faithful.

I've heard people say: "I know my friend is in bad shape; I really don't know what to say to them. So I haven't called."

Often, we don't have to say much. We can just listen. And we don't have to spend an eternity on the phone.

All of us have been hurt at some point—physically, emotionally and spiritually.

All of us can feel time slipping through our fingers. One way to battle the pain is to reach out to others, to let them know they matter.

In the morning, tell God, "I'm volunteering to work for You today, what can I do?"

Remember, it's not about doing big things . . . it's about doing something for someone else . . . and then watch God bless us and our moods in the process.

A teacher can change your life

I once had a teacher who changed my life.

Now that school is back in session, it's easy to focus on the boring teachers, the stressed teachers, the teachers who never should have become teachers in the first place.

And those thoughts wipe out all the good work done by so many teachers.

I'm a writer because of a teacher named Jim Muth. He taught honors English and was in charge of the school paper in the early 1970s when I was at Benedictine High School.

Mr. Muth saw something in me that I never knew was there. He believed I could write. He asked me several times to join the school paper.

Finally, I wrote a story about the freshman football team. There was magic seeing my name in print—and some kids reading my story.

That was in my freshman year. Mr. Muth also handed me a novel by Don Robertson, a former writer for the *Plain Dealer* and the old *Cleveland Press*.

The book was called *The Greatest Thing Since Sliced Bread*, and it was set in Cleveland. Mr. Muth told me to look for Robertson's column in the paper. The teacher's point was that here's a Cleveland guy who writes books—and you can do it, too.

While my parents loved newspapers and we had both Cleveland papers home delivered, I probably have written more books than were in my house while growing up.

So why write about this in a faith column?

Because I thank God for Mr. Muth. And for Father Dominic

Mondzelewski. And for Coach Augie Bossu, Phil Hodanbosi and so many other men who taught and coached me at Benedictine. And I thank God for an English professor named Susan Gorsky at Cleveland State.

She wrote scholarly works on Virginia Woolf. She also wrote romance novels for Harlequin. Unlike many academics I encountered, she thought writing sports for a newspaper was an admirable profession. And she encouraged me even when I wrote some very lousy fiction.

I have a friend who also is in journalism. She said her life changed at one of Cleveland's Senate schools.

A guidance counselor approached her and asked why she wasn't on the yearbook staff.

She had never even thought of it. The guidance counselor had seen some of her writing and set her up to talk to the teacher in charge of the yearbook.

"I doubt I would be a writer if that hadn't happened," she said.

Sometimes, our kids and other young people need to hear a story about a teacher who meant something to us. They need to know that there are good teachers.

Lots of them.

Psalm 32:8 reads: "I will instruct you and teach you in the way you should go. I will counsel you and watch over you."

This can apply to how God speaks and teaches people of faith in different ways.

But how about using that verse with a teacher who seems to have a good relationship with a young person in your life? Tell the teachers that you are praying for them—and do it.

Let the teacher know that she can have an impact. Or let him know about that important teacher in your life—and how he can do the same for your child.

Yes, teachers not only inspire—but they also can be inspired.

So often, we complain about the teachers who fall short.

But how often do we take time to not just talk to a teacher, but to lift that teacher up with our words?

Meet the Wayne Dawson
you don't know

You're Wayne Dawson. Sometimes you walk away from the Fox 8 television cameras and think, "How did this ever happen to me?"

It's been like that for more than 40 years at the same Cleveland station. You started as a part-timer; now you are in the prime morning news spot.

Wayne Dawson from East 128th Street on TV. Wayne Dawson, who remembers a time when you felt lost on the mean streets of Cleveland's East Side.

"Wayne Dawson, I watch you on TV all the time," someone often will tell you.

You smile. You pose for a picture. You shake hands. A little while later, you shake your head in pure wonder.

Then you go to your church. It's really God's church. But you are the pastor of Grace Tabernacle Baptist Church in Lyndhurst.

There are some Sunday mornings when you stand in the pulpit and preach the word of God . . . once in a while, you pause . . . just for a few seconds . . . and think, "Only God could have made this happen in my life."

That's part of the reason you decided to write your memoir, *The Seeds of Greatness Are Within You.* Your co-author was Deante Young, who did a nice job telling your story.

Why do the book now?

"Because people need to know they can succeed, even if they have a rough start," you say. "God can use you in a special way."

CALL ME GOGGLES

When you were in elementary school, you were the smart one—straight A's, good behavior in class. You wore glasses. Big round glasses with thick lenses.

"Hey, Goggles," some kids called you. It fit, because you were the star student. Your family believed you'd be the one to go to college. You'd be the one who did something special.

Yes, your family was working-class and worked hard. But there were problems. Your parents argued. Sometimes, it was physical. Once, you pulled your father off your mother. Sometimes when they screamed at each other, you felt sick. You wanted them to stop.

You wanted to disappear.

When you were in junior high, your father left home . . . sort of. He'd come back, then leave again.

"In junior high, I started hanging out with the wrong crowd," you say. "I started smoking weed and drinking wine. It was the 1970s. *Super Fly* and movies likes that—have lots of women, that was supposed to be the definition of a real man."

The guys on the street seemed to have it together. They were the cool ones.

Then one night, you hopped into a car. You had a bag of marijuana. Suddenly, there was a siren. Red flashing police lights. The driver pulled over. You hid the marijuana.

Turned out the car was stolen.

You kept telling the officer you had no idea that it was a stolen car. You thought it belonged to your friend. The officer drove you to the police station. He believed your story. He called your mother. She took you home.

No charges filed.

You look back and think, "What if I had been arrested? What if I had been charged with stealing the car? What if I was charged with a felony? What if I went to jail? Would I ever have had a TV career?"

WHO AM I?

You were the kid who continually was the super student and even had straight A's in the seventh grade . . .

Suddenly, that kid was gone. To the streets. To skipping school. To ignoring homework assignments.

"They say when you hang around nine fools, soon you'll be the 10th," you tell young people today.

Those were the days and nights of too much Wild Irish Rose and Boone's Farm. Too much marijuana.

Your mom knew it was a bad scene. But she was battling her own depression. Her marriage collapsed after she gave birth to your younger brother, William.

We need to stop here, to say that you're not the only star in the family. Brother William is now Judge William Dawson in East Cleveland.

"Only God . . . " you think when looking at William and yourself.

That's because you barely graduated from Shaw High. You had to go to summer school to earn your diploma. You knew you were better than that, but you really didn't know where you fit into the world.

HOW ABOUT COLLEGE?

You had a close friend named Corteze Brown. Veteran Cleveland basketball fans of a certain well-seasoned age might remember Brown as a star guard at Shaw High. His next stop was Cuyahoga Community College-Metro, where he averaged 34 points as a sophomore.

Because Brown was going to college, you decided to follow him. You were out of high school, washing dishes at Lutheran Medical Center and selling a little marijuana on the side. Your mom found a bag of weed. She was angry and hurt. Your heart was broken because her heart was broken.

You decided your minor-league drug-dealing days were over.

At CCC, you took remedial math to get your academics together. You loved sports, and wanted to become a sportswriter. You joined the school paper. You later wrote some stories for the Call & Post while still in junior college.

There was something about putting together a story, something about seeing your name in print . . .

The something was simple. You had a purpose. It was like you had put the goggles back on, and that overachieving, relentless working kid who had the great grades before high school was back.

When Corteze Brown received a basketball scholarship to Kent State, you followed. Brown thought he was headed to the NBA. You thought you were destined to write sports for the *Plain Dealer*.

HOW ABOUT BROADCASTING?

At Kent State, you took your collection of stories from the CCC school paper and the Call & Post to the newspaper office. You wanted to study journalism. They told you, "We have no room for you right now, come back next year."

You can't explain this part. You heard a voice . . . had a feeling . . . something was telling you not to quit, to go to the Music & Speech department. They embraced you. They put you on the school radio station doing sports reports. You had no idea exactly what you were doing. You had no formal training.

But there you were, on the air.

Next, you were doing some TV at Kent State. In the Cleveland market, you saw two African Americans doing the news: Leon Bibb and Bill Jacocks. If they could make it, why not you?

You spent four years at Kent State. You anchored the news program on the school TV station. You worked part time at WNIR, a commercial radio station known as WKNT back then. After graduating, you applied to several area TV stations. Nothing happened.

"But God . . . "

A friend of yours from Kent State named April Sutton knew Virgil Dominic, the legendary news director at WJW (TV-8) in Cleveland. She mentioned you. Dominic said for you to call. You did. He checked your work. He connected you with a minority broadcasters training program.

You worked on your English, smoothing out some of the "Black Dialect," as you call it. Your teacher was a speech therapist at Case Western Reserve. Within a month after leaving Kent State, you were on the air as a part-timer for TV-8.

Then it became full time as a news reporter.

When you were at Kent State, you pictured yourself doing this—being on Cleveland TV like Jacocks and Bibb. You wrote a list of goals and taped it to your mirror so you saw it each morning:

Wayne Dawson, TV newsman.

BEING PATIENT, PAYING DUES

You spent 10 years as a field reporter at Channel 8. Sometimes, you'd be on the set with Dick Goddard, Cleveland's most popular weatherman. You'd think, "I grew up watching him on TV. Now I'm here with him."

You knew racism was real. You dealt with it.

Stay strong. Stay with it. Stay focused. That was you in those days.

After 12 years, you became a weekend anchor. During this time, your work life was under control but your life away from the job needed work and discipline.

As a young man, you had three children with two women. You supported your children but had a hard time committing to marriage.

In 1996, your mother passed away at the age of 66. Something inside of you seemed to die, too. You knew for all your success on TV, something was missing. You had been dating LaVerne Reed on and off. You watched her take care of your mother in her final months.

A year later, you married LaVerne Reed on Aug. 29, 1997. You were 41 years old.

GET BACK TO WHAT MATTERS

When you were a kid, your mother took you to Bethany Baptist Church, where you loved to listen to the preaching of Pastor A.T. Rowan. You and your mom were living with your grandparents on Drexel Avenue on Cleveland's East Side. Your grandfather (Armfield Johnson) was a deacon.

You had church in you. And later, you realized you had more than that—you had the Holy Spirit guiding you. After getting married, you and LaVerne decided it was time to get back to church.

LaVerne heard of Bishop Joey Johnson, pastor of Akron's House of the Lord. You began attending that church. Even though you never joined, you took classes from Johnson—who became a spiritual mentor.

As you were given the morning anchor spot on Fox 8's news in 1999, you returned to your roots at Bethany Baptist.

It's a long story, but you became more involved in church, including personal education. In 2018, the morning man on Fox 8 was installed as the pastor of Grace Tabernacle Baptist Church. You wondered what Fox 8 would think of that. Well, station general manager Paul Perozeni gave you his blessing.

"If God can change my life and bring out the seeds of greatness within me, God can do it for you," is something you tell people.

STABILITY ON THE JOB

You have turned down offers from places such as Milwaukee and other Cleveland stations to stay at Fox 8.

You've survived nine general managers and eight news directors. The station has been sold seven times during your tenure. You've also worked with a dozen co-anchors over the decades. There have been 11 Emmy Awards, a Chuck Heaton Award and other honors.

It's also been 23 years of getting up at 2 a.m. to help anchor Cleveland's highest-rated morning news show. On the air from 5 a.m. to 9 a.m. Go to bed by 7:30 p.m.

You're 67 and you recently signed a new five-year contract. You and your brother—Judge William Dawson—lead The Dawson Foundation. It gives out scholarships and supports events such as Coats For Kids.

You and LaVerne have been married 25 years. You have a daughter, Danielle.

You remember writing your first Call & Post stories on a typewriter. In your early days of news, they advertised "film at 11." Film and typewriters seem like relics from the dinosaur age.

You think back to those days on the streets of East Cleveland. You think of how so many things could have gone wrong. You think of how you seemed to end up in broadcasting by accident, only it wasn't.

Finally, you think how "God has had his hand on me, even when I didn't know it."

A voice from the grave: 'Be not afraid!'

"I see in people what God wants me to see."

Those words coming from most other people would sound pretentious and strange. But they were spoken by Rob Sharkey, whose head was turned away from me. He was staring at me from the corner of his right eye.

"It's the only way I can see you," said Sharkey, whose left eye was completely and permanently shut.

Sharkey and I were talking about his vision of life as he was staring death in the eye due to cancer.

"I don't want this to be a story where people feel sorry for me," he said. "I don't feel sorry for me. I get frustrated sometimes, but I hate pity parties. I don't want one."

Sharkey was born three months premature, weighing only 2 pounds, 9 ounces. He suffered from cerebral palsy. He was permanently disabled from birth. He was unable to move his hands, legs or much of anything else.

Activities most of us take for granted were a chore for Sharkey and his helpers.

His life was an endless practice in patience. He had to wait for someone to help him do everything from eating to dressing to bathing . . .

You get the idea.

"But I really don't know anything else," he said. "It's been like this my entire life. How can I miss what I've never had?"

He also was classified as being blind.

"But I can see you from the corner of my right eye," he said. "I also can see you based on what you say and what we talk about."

Sharkey was saying God gave him the ability to see into another person's heart.

THE ODDS AGAINST HIM

I'd known Sharkey for the 4½ years that my "mama," Melva Hardison, has been at The Village of St. Edward nursing unit in Fairlawn. I first met Rob when he was sitting in a huge wheelchair near the front desk, talking with the receptionist, Mary Alice Randle, and others who came through the door.

It wasn't Sharkey who told me about his bachelor's degree from Kent State in psychology and then a master's degree in counseling. He followed that up with a master's degree in pastoral ministry from Ursuline College. It was some of his friends at the nursing home who told me.

Rob talked about his ability to comprehend and remember lectures from his teachers. He then spoke into a computer that turned his words into academic papers leading to advanced degrees.

Bob Price is Sharkey's uncle. He told the story of how Rob lived on campus at Kent State, attending classes in person. He had caretakers coming into his dorm room.

He had an extremely high IQ but sounded like your best buddy. He came across as an average guy who is friends with everyone. In her eulogy of Rob, his aunt, Cynthia, called him, "a human therapy dog. He just made you feel better after every visit."

That's how Sharkey wanted it.

"The odds were against me even surviving when they were feeding me with an eyedropper in the hospital," he said. "I wasn't ever supposed to be able to talk. Lots of people with cerebral palsy can't communicate like I can."

WHAT CAN YOU DO?

We sometimes hear motivational speakers with a message of making the most of what we have been given. Many of them look like they have a treasure chest of physical and intellectual gifts. We hear them, feel disconnected and think, "Nobody knows the troubles I've seen," as the old gospel song proclaims.

Sharkey knew more about troubles than most of us. He rarely complained. But he did have a message.

"I wish people wouldn't confuse a physical disability with a learning disability," he said. "Sometimes people talk about me— right in front of me—like I don't exist. They think I don't understand what is going on."

One of Sharkey's last requests is for everyone not to automatically put limitations on people with disabilities.

"See what they can do," he said. "Not what they can't do. When I was young, they wondered if I would be able to learn and talk. Would I have friends? I can do all those things."

His love of learning came from his parents, especially his mother, Alice Sharkey. She was a teacher in the Akron public system, once honored as the district's Teacher of the Year. Along with her husband, Bob Sharkey, the family led scouting groups for other disabled kids. They pushed for Rob to be "mainstreamed" in the school system before that was common.

She died in 2011 from lymphoma. That led to Sharkey leaving his West Akron home and moving into The Village of St. Edward.

DREAMLIKE GOD MOMENTS

When he was 16, Sharkey went on a Catholic retreat to a Sunrise Service.

"You know the song, 'Be Not Afraid'?" he asked. "I heard it that day. The lyrics went deep into my soul. It has stuck with me ever since."

Then Sharkey spoke the chorus from the song written by Father Bob Dufford:

Be not afraid
I go before you always
Come follow me
And I will give you rest.

Sharkey said those lyrics run through his mind whenever he feels fear tightening its grip on him.

Then Sharkey talked about a dream he had in 1996.

"I saw an angel," he said. "He said, 'I mean for you to be my messenger. Spread the gospel. You can use your voice and the computer to do it.' "

Sharkey said that was the only time he had a spiritual experience like that. It led to him teaching Bible studies, counseling people, and reflecting the love of God and Christ to others every day.

CONFESSION TIME

Sharkey spoke these words about five weeks ago. He was 58. After all his different health problems, he had been diagnosed with cancer.

We'd had casual conversations for years. We prayed together a few times.

When he was hit with congestion in the chest, it turned out he had cancer of the esophagus and lungs. It was too advanced for any major treatment.

We decided to talk for a story, one that I wanted to write before he died. After an hourlong discussion, he wanted to meet again before I did the story.

We never got together again.

My excuse is when I was visiting my "mama" several mornings each week, there were always people in Rob's room. He seemed to have hundreds of friends. Rather than butt in, I figured we'd have more time later. Basically, I wanted to do it on my schedule.

On June 10, I was at the Guardians game. I got a text from my wife reading, "Rob died."

I felt as if someone had slugged me in the stomach.

But I also thought of the words Rob heard from his angel: "I mean for you to be my messenger. Spread the gospel. You can use your voice and the computer to do it."

With this story, Rob is doing just that.

The Arizona desert, Springsteen and experiencing God away from the concrete

SALOME, ARIZONA—When I go to Arizona for spring training, I find myself doing more than watching baseball.

I'm drawn to the desert.

Once you get away from the cities, the strip malls and the interstates with as many as six lanes on each side (Yes, SIX!), you find something else.

But first, you see billboards advertising lawyers who want to sue someone for you. There are signs for casinos and places promising "the best weed in Arizona."

Too many cars. Too much smog. Not enough water.

But there also is the desert.

If you travel far enough and are willing drive down a gravel road—or hike a mile or two into the back country—you'll find it.

The quiet. The silence. The world as God made it.

In Luke 5:16, the Bible says: "(Jesus) withdrew himself into the wilderness, and prayed."

There are other passages in the Bible where "Jesus went to the mountainside to pray." (Luke 6:12).

When you read about Jesus heading to hills or the wilderness to pray, it's the desert of modern day Israel and Palestine.

NO CELL SERVICE

The desert . . .

In places such as California, Arizona and New Mexico, it seems as if the desert has lost out to car washes, warehouses, fast food joints—and concrete.

Lots and lots and lots of cement with never ending orange barrels and construction zones.

My wife, Roberta, and I went hiking at a place called the Harquahala Mountains, about 80 miles west of Phoenix. It's remote and rugged, and run by the Bureau of Land Management. The closest town is 20 long miles away.

We've been there a few times. Only once have we encountered people.

A few weeks ago, I wrote a column about our obsession with cellphones. They won't do you any good here, at least in terms of calls and texts.

But the camera. Pictures can tell the story.

A few hawks soared over head.

Some little lizards (perhaps 4 inches long) scampered by. One day hiking in another place called Skyline Regional Park near Buckeye, Arizona, we began counting lizards that ran across the trail. There were at least 20.

Counting lizards sounds dumb? Perhaps.

But they seemed to be happy dashing from rock to rock, scurrying through the sand, making what many would say this desolation their own. Hey, it's their land.

Psalm 134:1-2 reads: "Come, bless the LORD, all you servants of the LORD, who stand by night in the house of the LORD! Lift up your hands to the holy place and bless the LORD!"

If you're in the right frame of mind, the countless cacti rising seemingly out of angry rocks and thorny bushes transform the desert into a cathedral. No wonder Jesus and many prophets from the Old Testament came to places like this to pray.

SPRINGSTEEN WEIGHS IN

There are cacti staring down at you from on high . . . 10 feet . . . 20 feet . . . who knows how tall some of them are as their green arms seem to reach up to the sky. Charismatics would love it, seeing this as raising holy hands to the Lord.

This is tough country, where you can't build thousands of condos or quick loan businesses.

The sun beats down, there is no shade. It seems like it never rains, but when it does—the skies explode. Thunder booms. Lightning cracks. The earth shakes.

It's doesn't rain. It doesn't pour. The storm comes crashing down. The heavens aren't just weeping, they are wailing. The ground is baked so dry, the sudden outburst creates flash floods.

Then the unrelenting sun is back. You get a creepy feeling a snake is out there somewhere, with your name on its fangs. Those cute little cacti with the short arms? They don't have prickers. They don't have needles. They have little bayonets ready to slice right through your clothes.

When the desert is in this mood, I think of this line from Bruce Springsteen's *Western Skies*: "Here in the canyons . . . the desert don't give up the fight."

Yes, even a boy from New Jersey like Springsteen—or in my case, Cleveland—can relate to the desert on so many levels.

Then you walk along, and there it is . . . the desert is beginning to bloom. Red and yellow flowers open their mouths. It's like God smiling.

Then I think of Psalm 46:10: "Be still and know I am God."

And that's why Jesus and so many others went to the desert to pray.

Acknowledgments

I want to thank my book publisher David Gray. We've been working together since 2000. This is our 15th project together. I'm very grateful to Larry Pantages, my researcher and editor for this book and several others. I have been represented by Faith Hamlin for 38 years, even though my agent is only 35. It's amazing how math works when you appreciate someone.

I'm still extremely grateful for how the *Plain Dealer* and Cleveland.com have supported me as a faith writer. That's especially true of Skip Hall and David Campbell, who edit these columns each week. The faith column is also the most challenging story I write most weeks.

Then there is Roberta. We've been married 45 years, although she'll turn 31 in September. Some more miraculous math about the love of my life. She is the first reader of virtually all of my stories and books.

Finally, there is you, the reader. As I remind younger people in my business, without you (the reader), there would be no us (the writers/editors). You deserve the greatest thanks of all!

OTHER BOOKS BY TERRY PLUTO . . .

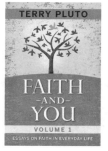

Faith and You Vol. 1
Essays on Faith in Everyday Life

Terry Pluto

Thoughtful essays on faith in everyday life from award-winning sportswriter Terry Pluto, who has also earned a reputation—and a growing audience—for his down-to-earth musings on spiritual subjects. Topics include choosing a church, lending money to friends, dealing with jerks, sharing your faith, visiting the sick, even planning a funeral.

Faith and You Vol. 2
More Essays on Faith in Everyday Life

Terry Pluto

More thoughtful essays by Terry Pluto ("the sportswriter who writes about faith"), based on his popular Plain Dealer column "Faith and You." These plain and personal musings discuss topics we all face in everday life: insults and what they really mean, prayers delayed or unanswered, sibling rivalry, relating to our fathers, losing a pet, and more.

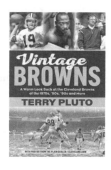

Vintage Browns
A Warm Look Back at the Cleveland Browns of the 1970s, '80s, '90s and More

Terry Pluto

Like a classic throwback jersey, this book recalls favorite players and moments from Cleveland Browns teams of the 1970s, '80s, '90s and more. Visit with Bernie Kosar, Ozzie Newsome, Brian Sipe, Marty Schottenheimer, Doug Dieken, Kevin Mack, Bill Belichik and others from days when the "Kardiac Kids" and the "Dawgs" ruled the old Stadium.

More at **www.grayco.com**

OTHER BOOKS BY TERRY PLUTO . . .

Browns Town 1964
The Cleveland Browns and the 1964
Championship

Terry Pluto

A nostalgic look back at the upstart AFC Cleveland
Browns' surprising 1964 championship victory over the
hugely favored Baltimore Colts. Profiles the colorful
players who made that season memorable, including
Jim Brown, Paul Warfield, Frank Ryan. Recreates an era
and a team for which pride was not just a slogan.

*"Pluto movingly reveals the substance of a mythic bond between men and a game,
a team and a city—and thus lays bare how present-day pro football has surrendered
its soul." – Kirkus Reviews*

Things I've Learned from Watching
the Browns
Terry Pluto

Veteran sports writer Terry Pluto asks Cleveland Browns
fans: Why, after four decades of heartbreak, teasing,
and futility, do you still stick with this team? Their
stories, coupled with Pluto's own insight and analysis,
deliver the answers. Like any intense relationship, it's
complicated. But these fans just won't give up.

*"For dedicated Browns fans [the book is] like leafing through
an old family photo album." – BlogCritics.com*

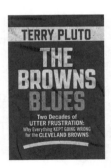

The Browns Blues
Two Decades of Utter Frustration: Why Everything
Kept Going Wrong for the Cleveland Browns

Terry Pluto

How could things go so wrong for so long? From their
return in 1999 through the winless 2017 season, the
Cleveland Browns had the worst record in the NFL. And
their fans had ulcers. Veteran sports columnist Terry
Pluto explains two decades of front-office upheaval and
frustrating football in this detailed, behind-the-scenes
analysis.

More at **www.grayco.com**

OTHER BOOKS BY TERRY PLUTO . . .

Glory Days in Tribe Town
The Cleveland Indians and Jacobs Field 1994–1997

Terry Pluto, Tom Hamilton

Relive the most thrilling seasons of Indians baseball in recent memory! Cleveland's top sportswriter teams up with the Tribe's veteran radio announcer and fans to share favorite stories from the first years of Jacobs Field, when a star-studded roster (Belle, Thome, Vizquel, Ramirez, Alomar, Nagy) and a sparkling ballpark captivated an entire city.

Our Tribe
A Baseball Memoir

Terry Pluto

A son, a father, a baseball team. Sportswriter Terry Pluto's memoir tells about growing up and learning to understand a difficult father through their shared love of an often awful baseball team. Baseball can be an important bridge across generations, sometimes the only common ground. This story celebrates the connection.

"A beautiful, absolutely unforgettable memoir." – Booklist

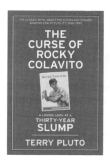

The Curse of Rocky Colavito
A Loving Look at a Thirty-Year Slump

Terry Pluto

A baseball classic. No sports fans suffered more miserable teams for more seasons than Indians fans of the 1960s, '70s, and '80s. Here's a fond and often humorous look back at "the bad old days" of the Tribe. The definitive book about the Indians of that generation, and a great piece of sports history writing.

"The year's funniest and most insightful baseball book." – Chicago Tribune

More at **www.grayco.com**

OTHER BOOKS BY TERRY PLUTO . . .

Vintage Cavs
A Warm Look Back at the Cavaliers of the Cleveland Arena and Richfield Coliseum Years

Terry Pluto

The Cleveland Arena and Richfield Coliseum are long gone, but they and the Cavaliers teams from 1970 to the 1990s come alive in this personal history by a sportswriter who was there as a young fan and later an NBA beat writer. From expansion team to the brink of greatness with Austin Carr, World B. Free, "Hot Rod" Williams, Mark Price, and others.

Joe Tait: It's Been a Real Ball
Stories from a Hall-of-Fame Sports Broadcasting Career

Terry Pluto, Joe Tait

Legendary broadcaster Joe Tait is like an old family friend to three generations of Cleveland sports fans. This book celebrates the inspiring career of "the Voice of the Cleveland Cavaliers" with stories from Joe and dozens of fans, colleagues, and players. Hits the highlights of a long career and also uncovers some touching personal details.

"An easy, fun book to read and will surely bring back good memories for Cleveland sports fans who listened to Tait's trademark calls since 1970."
– 20SecondTimeout.com

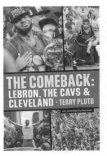

The Comeback: LeBron, the Cavs & Cleveland
How LeBron James Came Home and Brought a Championship to Cleveland

Terry Pluto

One of the greatest Cleveland sports stories ever! In this epic homecoming tale, LeBron James and the Cavaliers take fans on a roller coaster ride from despair to hope and, finally, to glory as the 2016 NBA champions. Terry Pluto tells how it all happened, with insightful analysis and behind-the-scenes details.

More at **www.grayco.com**